MW00465303

ACTIVITIES AND STUDY GUIDE

INTERNATIONAL BUSINESS

Dlabay **Scott**

SOUTH-WESTERN
™
THOMSON LEARNING

Australia • Canada • Mexico • Singapore • Spain • United Kingdom • United States

International Business
by Dlabay and Scott

Executive Editor
Eve Lewis

Project Manager
Enid Nagel

Production Manager
Patricia Matthews Boies

Marketing Manager
Nancy A. Long

Marketing Coordinator
Yvonne Patton-Beard

Editors
Darrell E. Frye and
Colleen A. Farmer

Print Buyer
Kevin L. Kluck

Cover and Internal Design
Bill Spencer

Editorial Assistant
Stephanie L. White

Compositor
Bill Lee

Printer
Mazer

Copyright © 2001 Delmar. South-Western Educational Publishing is an imprint of Delmar, a division of Thomson Learning, Inc. Thomson Learning™ is a trademark used herein under license.

ISBN: 0-538-69857-8

Printed in the United States of America
2 3 4 5 6 MZ 05 04 03 02

ALL RIGHTS RESERVED. No part of this work covered by copyright hereon may be reproduced or used in any form or by any means—graphic, electronic, or mechanical, including photocopying, recording, taping, Web distribution or information storage and retrieval systems—without the written permission of the publisher.

For permission to use material from this text or product, contact us by

Tel: (800) 730-2214
Fax: (800) 730-2215
Web: www.thomsonrights.com

For more information, contact South-Western Educational Publishing, 5101 Madison Road, Cincinnati, OH, 45227-1490. Or you can visit our Internet site at www.swep.com

International Divisions List

Asia (includes India):
Thomson Learning
60 Albert Street, #15-01
Albert Complex
Singapore 189969
Tel: 65 336-6411
Fax: 65 336-7411

Australia/New Zealand:
Nelson
102 Dodds Street
South Melbourne
Victoria 3205
Australia
Tel: 61 (0)3 9685-4111
Fax: 61 (0)3 9685-4199

Latin America:
Thomson Learning
Seneca 53
Colonia Polanco
11560 Mexico, D.F. Mexico
Tel: (525) 281-2906
Fax: (525) 281-2656

Canada:
Nelson
1120 Birchmount Road
Toronto, Ontario
Canada M1K 5G4
Tel: (416) 752-9100
Fax: (416) 752-8102

UK/Europe/Middle East/Africa:
Thomson Learning
Berkshire House
1680-173 High Holborn
London WC1V 7AA
United Kingdom
Tel: 44 (0)20 497-1422
Fax: 44 (0)20 497-1426

Spain (includes Portugal):
Paraninfo
Calle Magallanes 25
28015 Madrid
Espana
Tel: 34 (0)91 446-3350
Fax: 34 (0)91 445-6218

Table of Contents

Chapter 1 OUTLINE
We Live in a Global Economy

GLOBAL FOCUS: GLOBAL GOLDEN ARCHES

LESSON 1-1 THE FOUNDATION OF INTERNATIONAL BUSINESS

WHAT IS INTERNATIONAL BUSINESS?

WHY IS INTERNATIONAL BUSINESS IMPORTANT?

MATERIALS, PARTS, AND DEMAND

GLOBAL OPPORTUNITIES

IMPROVED POLITICAL RELATIONS

WHEN DID INTERNATIONAL BUSINESS START?

LESSON FEATURES
GLOBAL BUSINESS EXAMPLE: THE NORTH AMERICAN FREE TRADE AGREEMENT

E-COMMERCE IN ACTION: GLOBAL E-COMMERCE OPPORTUNITIES

LESSON 1-2 INTERNATIONAL BUSINESS BASICS

THE FUNDAMENTALS OF INTERNATIONAL TRADE

THE INTERNATIONAL BUSINESS ENVIRONMENT

INTERNATIONAL BUSINESS ENVIRONMENT FACTORS

Geographic Conditions

©South-Western Educational Publishing

Cultural and Social Factors

Political and Legal Factors

Economic Conditions

THE GLOBAL BUSINESS WORLD

INTERNATIONAL BUSINESS SKILLS

History

Geography

Foreign Language

Cultural Awareness Skills

Study Skills

THE GLOBAL CITIZEN, WORKER, AND CONSUMER

LESSON FEATURES
GLOBAL BUSINESS EXAMPLE: U.S. COMPANIES FACE TRADE BARRIERS

A QUESTION OF ETHICS

REGIONAL PERSPECTIVE: GEOGRAPHY: CANADA'S VAST NATURAL RESOURCES

 ©South-Western Educational Publishing

Lesson 1-1
The Foundation of International Business

LESSON QUIZ

Directions: For each of the following statements, if the statement is true, write a T on the answer line; if the statement is false, write an F on the answer line.

_____ 1. An example of domestic business is when a person living in Canada buys a product made in Germany.

_____ 2. An example of global dependency is when products are produced and used in the same country.

_____ 3. International business involves the buying and selling of products or services between countries.

_____ 4. Products sold by companies in the United States to customers in India are exports.

_____ 5. International trade usually reduces the product choices available to consumers.

Directions: For each of the following items, decide which choice best completes the statement. Write the letter that identifies your choice on the answer line.

_____ 6. Making, buying, and selling goods and services within a country is called
    A. international business.
    B. global dependency.
    C. domestic business.
    D. none of these

_____ 7. All business activities needed to create, ship, and sell goods and services across national borders are considered to be
    A. domestic business.
    B. international business.
    C. global dependency.
    D. none of these

_____ 8. A global dependency exists when
    A. massive crop failures require buying food from another country.
    B. a country buys tools from another country because it does not have the technology to make the tools.
    C. doctors travel to another country to provide healthcare because there is a shortage of medically-trained professionals in that country.
    D. all of these

_____ 9. Historically, international business
    A. is a relatively new concept made possible by communications technology.
    B. probably occurred as long as 15,000 years ago.
    C. declined when European countries created colonies on other continents.
    D. none of these

_____ 10. All of the following are benefits of international business except
    A. expanded business opportunities.
    B. increased sources of raw materials.
    C. decreased competition.
    D. improved political relationships

Activity 1 • Domestic or International

Directions: For each of the following situations, put a check mark in the appropriate column to indicate whether the situation is an example of domestic or international business.

		Domestic	International
1.	Products made in Canada are purchased by consumers in Egypt.		
2.	Workers live in Buffalo, New York, and work in Hamilton, Ontario.		
3.	Employees from northern California fly to Chicago for a sales meeting.		
4.	An investor from Australia buys stock in a U.S. corporation.		
5.	A business traveler from Utah buys apples grown in Washington to take back home.		
6.	French consumers purchase automobiles assembled in France that include parts from Japan, Italy, and Mexico.		

Activity 2 • International Business Examples

Directions: For each of the following terms or concepts, create an example that describes the situation listed. Your example can be one you have heard about or one you make up.

7. domestic business _____

_____

_____

8. international business _____

_____

_____

9. global dependency _____

_____

_____

Activity 3 • International Manufacturing

Directions: Products sold in developed countries may be manufactured in other, less developed countries, yet still have a domestic brand name. For this activity, examine the labels inside articles of clothing you own and complete the following chart. Guess the country for the brand name if it is not clearly indicated.

	Clothing Item	Brand Name	Brand Name Country	Country in Which Manufactured
10.				
11.				
12.				
13.				
14.				
15.				

 ©South-Western Educational Publishing

Lesson 1-2
International Business Basics

LESSON QUIZ

Directions: For each of the following statements, if the statement is true, write a T on the answer line; if the statement is false, write an F on the answer line.

_____ 1. A trade barrier makes it more difficult for a company to sell its products in other countries.

_____ 2. When consumers in the United States buy products made in Poland, they are buying imported goods.

_____ 3. Religious beliefs are not likely to influence international business activities.

_____ 4. International trade usually reduces the product choices available to consumers.

_____ 5. Expanded international business activities make different types of jobs available for workers.

_____ 6. Geography includes the study of the climate and terrain of a country.

Directions: For each of the following items, decide which choice best completes the statement. Write the letter that identifies your choice on the answer line.

_____ 7. Products that a seller sells in other countries are called
   A. imports.
   B. exports.
   C. trade barriers.
   D. none of these

_____ 8. Products that a buyer buys from businesses in other countries are called
   A. imports.
   B. exports.
   C. trade barriers.
   D. none of these

_____ 9. Free trade among countries can be restricted by
   A. import taxes.
   B. trade barriers.
   C. import quotas.
   D. all of these

_____ 10. Which of the following statements is an example of a cultural factor that can affect international business?
   A. The weather is too hot for selling ice cream products without refrigeration units.
   B. Consumer protection laws require expensive packaging.
   C. The major religion prohibits the use of alcohol in any food products.
   D. none of these

_____ 11. Which of the following statements about international business and individual citizens is *not* true.
   A. Individual decisions may affect people in other parts of the world.
   B. International business usually decreases career opportunities.
   C. Individual shopping habits have no effect on international business.
   D. International competition usually results in fewer product choices for individuals.

Activity 1 • Analyzing International Business Data

Directions: Use the following table of import and export data to answer the questions.

Import and Export Data for Selected Countries (in billions of U.S. dollars)		
Country	**Exports**	**Imports**
Canada	208.6	194.4
France	275.0	256.0
Japan	421.0	339.8
Mexico	110.4	109.8
United Kingdom	268.0	283.5
United States	625.1	822.0

1. Which country has the largest amount of exports?_____

_____

2. Which country has the smallest amount of imports?_____

_____

3. What is the total export amount and import amount for the North American countries listed? _____

_____

4. What is the total export amount and import amount for the European countries listed? _____

_____

5. By how much do imports exceed exports for the United States? _____

_____

6. By how much do exports exceed imports for Japan? _____

_____

7. How many times larger is Japan's import amount than Mexico's import amount? _____

_____

8. What percentage of the United States' export amount is the French export amount? _____

_____

9. If Canada's exports grow to $250 billion the following year, what would be the percentage increase?

_____

_____

10. If Mexico's imports were $91.3 billion in the previous period, what is the percentage increase? _____

_____

_____

 ©South-Western Educational Publishing

Activity 2 • Analyzing International Business Influences

Directions: For each of the following, place a check mark in the appropriate column to tell if the situation is an example of a cultural and social condition, a political and legal condition, or an economic condition. Then describe how the situation could affect the business activities of a company.

	Cultural and Social	Political and Legal	Economic
11. A company that sells candy discovers it cannot advertise its product on television programs aimed at children in a certain country.			
12. A computer manufacturer learns that in a country in which it plans to sell only a few companies have the financial resources to purchase its equipment.			
13. A food company is unable to sell its product in a country in which consumers believe the taste of the item is disgusting.			
14. A manager greets foreign customers by calling them by their first names, a practice that is not appropriate until the parties are better acquainted.			

Part 3 • Developing Geography Skills

Directions: Based on your knowledge and the use of other resources, indicate the following items on the map provided on page 10.

15. Place an X on the area where you live.

16. Canada, Japan, and Mexico are three major trading partners of the United States. Place a dollar sign ($) on each of these three countries.

17. Draw a dotted line between the United States and Europe.

18. More people live in China than in any other country. Place a star (*) on China.

19. South Africa is the major source of diamonds for the world. Draw a diamond (◇) on South Africa.

20. Tropical fruits, such as bananas, are grown in Central America. Circle Central America on the map.

21. The Middle East is a major source of oil for the world. Place a check mark (✔) on this area of the world.

22. Draw a solid line to show the water route used for shipping products from South America to Australia.

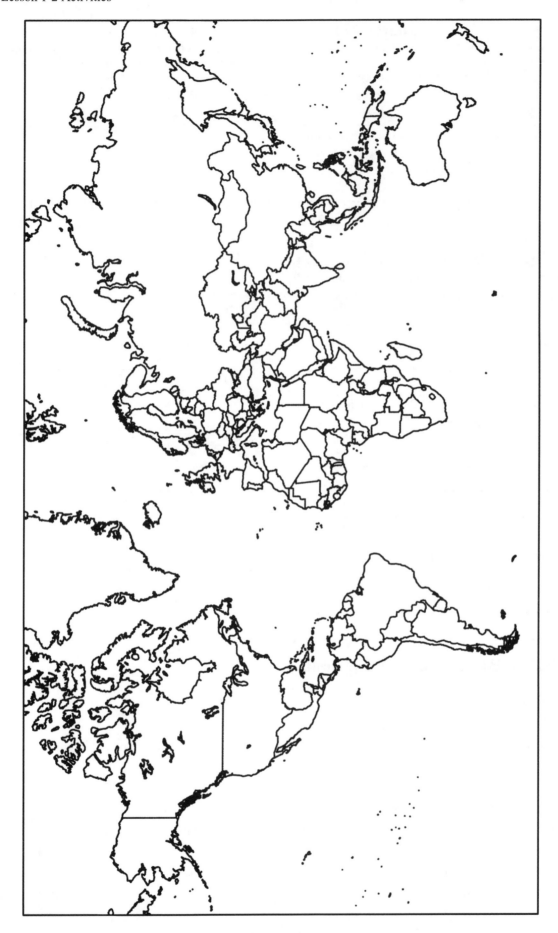

 ©South-Western Educational Publishing

Chapter 2 OUTLINE
Our Global Economy

GLOBAL FOCUS: A NEW ECONOMIC DIRECTION FOR MEXICO

LESSON 2-1 ECONOMICS AND DECISION MAKING

THE BASIC ECONOMIC PROBLEM

MAKING ECONOMIC DECISIONS

THE DECISION-MAKING PROCESS

DECISION MAKING IN ACTION

LESSON 2-2 BASICS OF ECONOMICS

PRICE-SETTING ACTIVITIES

CHANGING PRICES

LESSON FEATURE
COMMUNICATION ACROSS BORDERS: DISAPPEARING LANGUAGES

LESSON 2-3 ECONOMIC SYSTEMS

ECONOMIC RESOURCES SATISFY NEEDS

Natural Resources

Human Resources

Capital Resources

TYPES OF ECONOMIC SYSTEMS

COMMAND ECONOMIES

MARKET ECONOMIES

MIXED ECONOMIES

LESSON FEATURES
GLOBAL BUSINESS EXAMPLE: FACTORS OF PRODUCTION FOR FAST-FOOD COMPANIES

GLOBAL BUSINESS EXAMPLE: PUBLIC SERVICES GOING PRIVATE

LESSON 2-4 ACHIEVING ECONOMIC DEVELOPMENT

DEVELOPMENT FACTORS

TYPES OF DEVELOPMENT

INDUSTRIALIZED COUNTRIES

LESS-DEVELOPED COUNTRIES

DEVELOPING COUNTRIES

LESSON FEATURE
GLOBAL BUSINESS EXAMPLE: TYPES OF INFRASTRUCTURE

LESSON 2-5 RESOURCES SATISFY NEEDS

THE ECONOMICS OF FOREIGN TRADE

MEASURING ECONOMIC PROGRESS

MEASURE OF PRODUCTION

INTERNATIONAL TRADE ACTIVITY

OTHER ECONOMIC MEASUREMENTS

LESSON FEATURES
E-COMMERCE IN ACTION: INTERNATIONAL DOMAIN NAMES

REGIONAL PERSPECTIVE: THE FOUNDER OF BLACK HISTORY MONTH

Lesson 2-1
Economics and Decision Making

LESSON QUIZ

Directions: For each of the following statements, if the statement is true, write a T on the answer line; if the statement is false, write an F on the answer line.

_____ 1. Scarcity refers to not having enough resources to fulfill everyone's needs.

_____ 2. Most people do not have the opportunity to make economic decisions.

_____ 3. The study of economics can explain why business managers make certain decisions.

_____ 4. The first step of the decision-making process is to define the problem.

_____ 5. When a decision is made the opportunity cost should usually be greater than the benefits of the decision.

_____ 6. The six-step decision-making process is only for making business decisions.

Directions: For each of the following items, decide which choice best completes the statement. Write the letter that identifies your choice on the answer line.

_____ 7. Economics is the study of how
   A. decisions are made using six steps.
   B. limited resources are used to satisfy unlimited wants and needs.
   C. individuals make decisions about buying products.
   D. none of these

_____ 8. If you decide to get a full-time job after graduating from high school instead of going to college, the opportunity cost of the decision is
   A. the salary from your job.
   B. the money saved on college tuition.
   C. the loss of a college education.
   D. none of these

_____ 9. When you evaluate the alternatives in the decision-making process, you
   A. analyze the advantages and disadvantages of each alternative.
   B. decide what needs to be done to put a decision into action.
   C. determine the different ways your problem can be solved.
   D. all of these

_____ 10. After you take action on a choice in the decision-making process, it is important to review the decision because
   A. changed circumstances may require a change in the decision.
   B. a different decision may need to be made.
   C. you may have made an error in defining the original problem.
   D. all of these

Activity 1 • Identifying the Steps of the Decision-Making Process

Directions: List the following steps of the decision-making process in the correct order. Then, provide an example of the use of these steps by a person or a business.

Make a Choice   Evaluate the Alternatives
Define the Problem   Take Action on the Choice
Review the Decision   Identify the Alternatives

	Steps in the Decision-Making Process	Example of the Step
1.	Define the Problem	
2.	Identify the Alternatives	
3.	Evaluate the Alternatives	
4.	Make a Choice	
5.	Take Action on the Choice	
6.	Review the Decision	

Activity 2 • Identifying Alternatives

Directions: For each of the following problems, identify at least three different solutions.

7. You have been accepted at the college of your choice, but between your savings and what your parents can afford, you do not have enough money for tuition, books, and expenses.

   _____

   _____

   _____

8. Your company's new product has been so successful that you need to manufacture more to satisfy customer wants.

   _____

   _____

   _____

9. Sales of your product have slowed and you need to create new interest in the product to increase sales.

   _____

   _____

   _____

10. Your factory assembly line is often stopped because of equipment breakdown and it is beginning to affect sales.

   _____

   _____

   _____

 ©South-Western Educational Publishing

Lesson 2-2
Basics of Economics

LESSON QUIZ

Directions: For each of the following statements, if the statement is true, write a T on the answer line; if the statement is false, write an F on the answer line.

_____ 1. The point at which supply and demand are equal is the opportunity cost.

_____ 2. If the supply of an item decreases, the price usually goes up.

_____ 3. On a graph of supply and demand, the market price is where the supply line and the demand line intersect.

_____ 4. Continually rising prices are one sign of a healthy economy.

_____ 5. When supply exceeds demand, demand-pull inflation occurs.

Directions: For each of the following items, decide which choice best completes the statement. Write the letter that identifies your choice on the answer line.

_____ 6. If a technological change makes a product obsolete, usually
   A. demand will increase.
   B. demand will decrease.
   C. supply will increase.
   D. none of these

_____ 7. The relationship between price and the amount of a good that consumers are willing and able to purchase is
   A. supply.
   B. demand.
   C. equilibrium price.
   D. none of these

_____ 8. If consumers want more of a good than the amount supplied
   A. prices will decrease.
   B. prices will increase.
   C. supply will decrease.
   D. none of these

_____ 9. The relationship between price and the amount of a good that businesses are willing and able to make available is
   A. supply.
   B. demand.
   C. equilibrium price.
   D. none of these

_____ 10. The type of inflation that may result when a government prints too much money or people increase their borrowing to be able to make purchases is
   A. demand-pull inflation.
   B. cost-push inflation.
   C. government inflation.
   D. none of these

Activity 1 • Graphing Supply and Demand

Directions: Use the supply and demand information in the table below to create a graph of supply and demand. Label the graph clearly. Then answer the questions that follow.

Price	Units Supplied	Units Demanded
$10	100	600
$20	200	500
$30	300	400
$40	400	300
$50	500	200
$60	600	100

1. What is the market price on your graph above? _____

   _____

2. If the quantities demanded at each price decreased, how would that affect the graph for Demand? _____

   _____

   _____

3. If the quantities demanded at each price decreased by 100, what would be the new market price? (Hint: Draw a new Demand line on your graph.) _____

©South-Western Educational Publishing

Lesson 2-3
Economic Systems

LESSON QUIZ

Directions: For each of the following statements, if the statement is true, write a T on the answer line; if the statement is false, write an F on the answer line.

_____ 1. Water is an example of a natural resource.

_____ 2. The three factors of production are natural resources, infrastructure, and capital.

_____ 3. Capital resources are expensive and usually used over a period of several years.

_____ 4. Economic systems are categorized on how resources are owned and the size of the economy.

_____ 5. In market economies, most economic decisions are made by the government.

_____ 6. An industry that undergoes privatization is changed from private ownership to government ownership.

Directions: For each of the following items, decide which choice best completes the statement. Write the letter that identifies your choice on the answer line.

_____ 7. Capital resources include
   A. gold, silver, and other minerals.
   B. buildings, money, and equipment.
   C. factories, mines, and talented personnel.
   D. none of these

_____ 8. An economy in which an individual may own and run a private business to make a profit, with little government involvement with business is a
   A. communist economy.
   B. command economy.
   C. mixed economy.
   D. none of these

_____ 9. Private property, profit motive, and a free, competitive marketplace are characteristics of a
   A. command economy.
   B. market economy.
   C. mixed economy.
   D. none of these

_____10. Another term for a free enterprise system is
   A. communism.
   B. capitalism.
   C. socialism.
   D. none of these

Activity 1 • Identifying Factors of Production

Directions: List the factors of production that would be needed to produce the following items.

1. Hamburger and fries

   Natural resources: _____

   _____

   Human resources: _____

   _____

   Capital: _____

   _____

2. School

   Natural resources: _____

   _____

   Human resources: _____

   _____

   Capital: _____

   _____

3. Computer and software

   Natural resources: _____

   _____

   Human resources: _____

   _____

   Capital: _____

   _____

Activity 2 • Analyzing Economic Systems

Directions: Place a check mark in the appropriate column(s) to tell if the situation is characteristic of a command economy, a market economy, or a mixed economy.

		Command Economy	Mixed Economy	Market Economy
4.	Consumers have freedom of choice in the marketplace.			
5.	Blends government involvement and private consumer choice.			
6.	Central planning committee makes most economic decisions.			
7.	Factors of production are owned by individuals and private companies.			
8.	Most basic industries are owned and operated by the government.			
9.	Individuals have the chance to be rewarded for risk taking.			
10.	An economy that is also referred to as socialism.			
11.	Government selects who gets what job.			

©South-Western Educational Publishing

Lesson 2-4
Achieving Economic Development

LESSON QUIZ

Directions: For each of the following statements, if the statement is true, write a T on the answer line; if the statement is false, write an F on the answer line.

_____ 1. The main influences on a country's level of economic development are literacy level, technology, and agricultural dependency.

_____ 2. Literacy level is an important measure of a country's level of economic development because better-educated citizens can usually produce more goods and services of high quality.

_____ 3. A country with a large agricultural base is usually more economically developed than one with a large manufacturing base.

_____ 4. Infrastructure refers to how many buildings a country has.

_____ 5. Less developed countries usually have a high infant death rate because of lack of housing, food, and health care.

_____ 6. Developing countries have an economic development somewhere between that of a less developed country and an industrialized country.

_____ 7. A less-developed country is a country with low economic wealth and an emphasis on agriculture or mining.

Directions: For each of the following terms, write the letter identifying the term next to its definition.

      A. developing country

      B. industrialized country

      C. infrastructure

      D. less-developed country (LDC)

_____ 8. A nation's transportation, communications, and utility systems.

_____ 9. A country with strong business activity that is usually the result of advanced technology and a highly educated population.

_____ 10. A country that is evolving from less developed to industrialized.

_____ 11. A country with little economic wealth and an emphasis on agriculture or mining.

Activity 1 • Analyzing International Business News

Directions: Locate information related to a developing or less-developed country. Use a recent newspaper or magazine article, web site, or television or radio news report. If the source is a printed article, attach a copy to this page if possible. Then answer the following questions.

1. Source of information _____

_____

2. Date of article or report _____

3. How would you rate the reliability of your source? Why? _____

_____

_____

_____

4. What are the main facts in the article or news report? _____

_____

_____

_____

_____

5. How do you know whether the country is a developing or less-developed country? _____

_____

_____

_____

_____

_____

6. What is the country doing to improve its economic development? _____

_____

_____

_____

_____

7. What kind of assistance is the country receiving from other countries or organizations? _____

_____

_____

_____

_____

8. What recommendations would you make for the country to improve its economic development? _____

_____

_____

_____

Lesson 2-5
● # Resources Satisfy Needs

LESSON QUIZ
Directions: For each of the following statements, if the statement is true, write a T on the answer line; if the statement is false, write an F on the answer line.

_____ 1. An absolute advantage exists when a country can produce a good or service at a lower cost than other countries.

_____ 2. When a country has an absolute advantage in more than one area, it will maximize its economic wealth by focusing on the area in which it is relatively more efficient.

_____ 3. The gross domestic product of France would not include products manufactured in England using French resources.

_____ 4. When two countries are being compared, the one with the higher total GNP has the stronger economy.

_____ 5. A trade surplus exists when a country's imports are greater than its exports.

Directions: For each of the following items, decide which choice best completes the statement. Write the letter that identifies your choice on the answer line.

_____ 6. The consumer price index shows
   A. how many consumer products a particular foreign currency can purchase.
   B. price levels for various products and services.
   C. the total price of the goods and services produced by a country in a period of time.
   D. none of these

_____ 7. The unemployment rate is an indicator of a country's economic situation because
   A. people not earning an income reduce the flow of money in circulation.
   B. fewer goods and services are produced when there is high unemployment.
   C. a high rate can cause other people to lose their jobs.
   D. all of these

_____ 8. South Africa has a large percentage of the world's diamond deposits. This is an example of
   A. comparative advantage.
   B. absolute advantage.
   C. a developing country.
   D. none of these

_____ 9. Balance of trade is calculated by
   A. dividing total exports by total imports.
   B. dividing total imports by total exports.
   C. multiplying total imports by total exports.
   D. none of these

_____10. Per capita GDP is a better measure of a nation's economic development than total GDP because
   A. it shows how wealthy each person in the country is.
   B. it gives a better comparison between countries of different population sizes.
   C. it shows how the unemployment rate affects GDP.
   D. none of these

Activity 1 • Calculating International Economic Data

Directions: Answer each of the following questions. Show your calculations.

1. The GNP of a country is $204 billion, and the country has a population of 24 million people. What is the
   per capita GNP? _____

   _____

   _____

   _____

2. Estimate (do not perform an exact calculation) the per capita GNP of a country with $617 billion GDP
   and a population of 300 million people. _____

   _____

   _____

   _____

   _____

3. If a country has $45 billion in exports for a year and $42 billion in imports, what is the balance of trade?
   Is it favorable or unfavorable? _____

   _____

   _____

   _____

4. If the country in Question #3 expects a 25% increase in imports and a 10% increase in exports next year,
   what will be the expected balance of trade next year? Is it favorable or unfavorable? _____

   _____

   _____

   _____

5. A country has a foreign debt of $450 million. In the current year, the country imports $375 million of
   goods and services and exports $367 million. What is the country's new foreign debt? _____

   _____

   _____

   _____

6. A country of 1.5 million people has an unemployment rate of 11.2%. _____

   _____

   _____

   _____

  ©South-Western Educational Publishing

Chapter 3 OUTLINE
Cultural Influences on Global Business

GLOBAL FOCUS: WALT DISNEY COMPANY ADJUSTS TO FRANCE

LESSON 3-1 CULTURE AROUND THE WORLD

CULTURAL INFLUENCES IN INTERNATIONAL BUSINESS

THE SUBCULTURES WITHIN A SOCIETY

INFLUENCES OF CULTURES AND SUBCULTURES

SUBCULTURE OF U.S. BUSINESS

VARIATIONS IN BUSINESS SUBCULTURES WORLDWIDE

LESSON FEATURE
GLOBAL BUSINESS EXAMPLE: THE SAME OR DIFFERENT?

LESSON 3-2 CULTURAL AND SOCIAL ORGANIZATIONS

FAMILY RELATIONSHIPS

FAMILY UNITS

FAMILY-WORK RELATIONSHIPS

SOCIETY'S INSTITUTIONS

EDUCATION

GENDER ROLES

©South-Western Educational Publishing

MOBILITY

CLASS SYSTEM

LESSON FEATURE
A QUESTION OF ETHICS: BLOOD IS THICKER THAN WATER

LESSON 3-3 COMMUNICATION ACROSS CULTURES

LANGUAGE DIFFERENCES

LEARNING A SECOND LANGUAGE

DIRECT AND INDIRECT COMMUNICATION

NONVERBAL COMMUNICATION

Body Language

Appearance

Eye Contact

Touching

Personal Space

Color

Numbers

 ©South-Western Educational Publishing

Emblems

Smells

LESSON FEATURES

GLOBAL BUSINESS EXAMPLE: SAYING "NO" THE JAPANESE WAY

COMMUNICATION ACROSS BORDERS: THE CANADIAN HANDSHAKING CODE

LESSON 3-4 VALUES AROUND THE WORLD

VALUES VARY AMONG CULTURES

INDIVIDUALISM AND COLLECTIVISM

TECHNOLOGY

LEADERSHIP, POWER, AND AUTHORITY

RELIGION

TIME

ADJUSTING TO CULTURAL DIFFERENCES

ETHNOCENTRISM

REACTIONS TO CULTURAL DIFFERENCES

LESSON FEATURES
GLOBAL BUSINESS EXAMPLE: SAUDI-ARABIA PROTECTS ITS OWN CULTURAL VALUES

REGIONAL PERSPECTIVE: CULTURE: FRENCH CUISINE

Lesson 3-1
Culture Around the World

LESSON QUIZ

Directions: For each of the following statements, if the statement is true, write a T on the answer line; if the statement is false, write an F on the answer line.

_____ 1. A culture is the sum of a group's way of life.

_____ 2. All aspects of a particular culture are usually taught in homes, schools, religious institutions, and the workplace.

_____ 3. It is usually possible to learn all about a culture by examining people's behavior, appearance, and the culture's literature, art, and music.

_____ 4. Most people are members of more than one subculture.

_____ 5. Business subcultures around the world have similar values, beliefs, and assumptions.

_____ 6. Each business subculture has its own mind-set.

_____ 7. Canada and the United States have identical business subcultures.

Directions: For each of the following items, decide which choice best completes the statement. Write the letter that identifies your choice on the answer line.

_____ 8. A culture is
   A. a system of learned, shared, unifying, and interrelated beliefs, values, and assumptions.
   B. usually logical and reasonable to people outside the culture.
   C. shared willingly with outsiders.
   D. none of these

_____ 9. A high school student
   A. is a member of several different subcultures.
   B. can be a member of any subculture.
   C. is usually too inexperienced to have developed any cultural baggage.
   D. none of these

_____10. Business subcultures would probably be very similar in
   A. France, Egypt, and Chile.
   B. the U.K., U.S.A, and Italy.
   C. Argentina, Chile, and Venezuela.
   D. none of these

Activity 1 • Interpreting Subculture Jargon

Directions: Interpret the following sayings by explaining what each means in the U.S. business subculture. As you do so, you will learn about some of the guiding principles of the U.S. business subculture.

1. There's more than one way to skin a cat. _____

_____

_____

_____

2. A stitch in time saves nine. _____

_____

_____

_____

3. The squeaky wheel gets the grease. _____

_____

_____

4. There is always room at the top. _____

_____

_____

5. You've made your bed; now sleep in it. _____

_____

_____

Activity 2 • Describing a Subculture

Directions: Consider a group of people with whom you associate. You may choose an organized group such as a team or club or religious group, or simply a group of friends you spend a lot of time with. Describe this group as a subculture by supplying the following information about the group.

6. What is the average age of the group members? _____

7. What are the characteristics of members of this subculture? _____

_____

_____

8. What are two beliefs of this subculture that are not shared by most other subcultures? _____

_____

_____

9. What are two actions that the subculture would disapprove of? _____

_____

_____

 ©South-Western Educational Publishing

Lesson 3-2
Culture and Social Organizations

LESSON QUIZ

Directions: For each of the following statements, if the statement is true, write a T on the answer line; if the statement is false, write an F on the answer line.

_____ 1. Extended families are very common in developed countries.

_____ 2. Family and business ties are weak in the United States and strong in Mexico.

_____ 3. One aspect of mobility is the willingness to relocate to another location for better employment.

_____ 4. Although it was not always true in the past, today women can participate equally with men in the workplace in all countries.

_____ 5. A culture that values education for all its members has a business advantage over those that do not.

_____ 6. In a country with a strong class system, it is relatively difficult to change your class level.

Directions: For each of the following items, decide which choice best completes the statement. Write the letter that identifies your choice on the answer line.

_____ 7. In a culture with strong business and family ties
   A. several members of a family may work in the same business.
   B. family members are usually promoted first in a family-owned business.
   C. protecting a family member is sometimes more important than a good business decision.
   D. all of these

_____ 8. Education, occupation, and income are factors that may determine
   A. mobility.
   B. gender roles.
   C. class level.
   D. none of these

_____ 9. Members of a society are most likely to have good educational opportunities in
   A. a developing country.
   B. a less developed country.
   C. an industrialized economy.
   D. none of these

_____ 10. In most cultures the belief about gender roles is that
   A. both males and females work outside the home.
   B. males are the primary workers outside the home.
   C. females may work outside the home but are not the primary support of the family.
   D. none of these

_____ 11. A situation in which parents, children, and other relatives live together is
   A. a nuclear family.
   B. an extended family.
   C. family class system.
   D. none of these

Activity 1 • Analyzing Society's Institutions

Directions: Locate information related to education, gender roles, mobility, or class system in another country. Use a recent newspaper or magazine article, web site, or television or radio news report. If the source is a printed article, attach a copy to this page if possible. Then answer the following questions.

1. Source of information _____

_____

2. Date of article or report _____

3. How would you rate the reliability of your source? Why? _____

_____

_____

_____

4. What are the main facts in the article or news report? _____

_____

_____

_____

_____

_____

5. How does this country's institution differ from yours? _____

_____

_____

_____

_____

_____

6. What effect does this institution have on the country's domestic business? _____

_____

_____

_____

_____

_____

7. What effect does this institution have on the country's international business? _____

_____

_____

_____

_____

©South-Western Educational Publishing

Lesson 3-3
Communication Across Cultures

LESSON QUIZ

Directions: For each of the following statements, if the statement is true, write a T on the answer line; if the statement is false, write an F on the answer line.

_____ 1. Spanish is not an important business language.

_____ 2. The major advantage of English as a language for conducting international business is that it takes fewer words to send a message than some other languages.

_____ 3. Since English is the major language in international business, it is not very useful to learn another language.

_____ 4. In a high-context culture, language is very direct and words are taken literally.

_____ 5. In high-context cultures, business people make a serious mistake if they cause a customer personal embarrassment.

_____ 6. The meanings of body language are universal.

Directions: For each of the following items, decide which choice best completes the statement. Write the letter that identifies your choice on the answer line.

_____ 7. Nonverbal communication
   A. includes body language, color, and smells.
   B. includes written language but not spoken language.
   C. includes e-mail.
   D. none of these

_____ 8. In international business activities
   A. people from the U.S. need more personal space than people from many other countries.
   B. personal space requirements are a form of nonverbal communication.
   C. it is important to make people from other cultures comfortable by respecting their personal space requirements.
   D. all of these

_____ 9. In the United States brides traditionally dress in white for a wedding but in China they dress in red. This is an example of
   A. body language.
   B. nonverbal communication.
   C. contexting.
   D. none of these

_____ 10. All of the following are examples of nonverbal communication except
   A. wearing black to a funeral in the United States.
   B. shaking hands when you meet a new business associate.
   C. introducing your husband to a coworker at a business dinner.
   D. wearing a suit to a job interview

Activity 1 • Interpreting Nonverbal Communication

Directions: For each of the following situations, describe what the nonverbal communication means. Then suggest an appropriate response.

1. You are interviewing Susan Smith for a job with your company. Susan is now leaning closer as you speak.

   Meaning: _____

   _____

   Response: _____

   _____

2. You are making a sales presentation to Mark Atilo, who is playing with a pen and fidgeting.

   Meaning: _____

   _____

   Response: _____

   _____

3. You are trying to persuade a male friend to go to a particular movie with you, but he is frowning.

   Meaning: _____

   _____

   Response: _____

   _____

4. You are selling your house and showing it to the Perez family who seem to like the house. You quote a price and Mr. Perez narrows his eyes and crosses his arms.

   Meaning: _____

   _____

   Response: _____

   _____

5. As you describe your company's new product, Fuji Nitobe nods and jots down a few notes.

   Meaning: _____

   _____

   Response: _____

   _____

6. You are on a new car lot listening to Sandra Gerber describe the features of a car. She won't look you in the eye, although she glances at you once or twice.

   Meaning: _____

   _____

   Response: _____

   _____

 ©South-Western Educational Publishing

Lesson 3-4
Values Around the World

LESSON QUIZ

Directions: For each of the following statements, if the statement is true, write a T on the answer line; if the statement is false, write an F on the answer line.

_____ 1. No culture has both individualism and collectivism.

_____ 2. Technology threatens the way of life of some cultural groups.

_____ 3. Religious beliefs dominate business practices in the United States even though there are several major religions.

_____ 4. All countries welcome technology as a way of improving the standard of living.

_____ 5. Clock time is generally viewed as unimportant in industrialized countries such as Canada.

_____ 6. Reverse culture shock is a normal reaction to returning home after a lengthy stay abroad.

Directions: For each of the following items, decide which choice best completes the statement. Write the letter that identifies your choice on the answer line.

_____ 7. Collectivism is characterized by
   A. self-reliance.
   B. consensus or group agreement.
   C. selfishness.
   D. none of these

_____ 8. The attitudes of business subcultures toward technology
   A. are usually positive in developed countries.
   B. are not affected by religious beliefs.
   C. are positive in India where people are relieved from performing menial tasks.
   D. none of these

_____ 9. In authoritarian countries such as China
   A. requests to share authority are not welcome by the leaders.
   B. leaders modify decisions based on feedback from citizens.
   C. leadership, power, and authority are concentrated in the hands of a few older leaders.
   D. none of these

_____ 10. Reverse culture shock is
   A. a reaction to becoming reacquainted with your own culture after having accepted another culture.
   B. frustration in adapting to a culture other than your own.
   C. highly unusual when returning to your own culture.
   D. none of these

Activity 1 • Times Around the World

The world is divided into 24 time zones. The time zone that includes the prime meridian is called Greenwich mean time or GMT. Times throughout the world are calculated from GMT. Locations in time zones to the left of the prime meridian have earlier times, and locations in time zones to the right of the prime meridian have later times. How much earlier or later the time is than GMT depends on how many time zones the location is from the one including the prime meridian. For example, if it is noon in London, which has GMT, it is 1 p.m. in Paris. Paris is located one time zone to the right of the prime meridian.

Directions: Using the time-zone map on pages 582-583 of your text book, for questions 1-8 determine what time it is in the following cities if it is noon GMT. Then answer the remaining questions. Show all your calculations.

1. Tokyo, Japan _____

_____

2. Brasilia, Brazil _____

_____

3. Kananga, Dem. Rep of the Congo _____

_____

4. Honolulu, Hawaii, U.S.A. _____

_____

5. Paris, France _____

_____

6. New York City, New York, U.S.A. _____

_____

7. Bombay, India _____

_____

8. Halifax, Nova Scotia, Canada _____

_____

9. What time should you call from your Los Angeles office to talk to a supplier in Spain at 2 p.m.? _____

_____

_____

10. What time will you arrive in Chicago on a 9-hour flight departing London at 7 a.m.? _____

_____

_____

11. What time should you login in Anchorage, Alaska to watch an Internet broadcast of a concert starting at

8 p.m. in Moscow? _____

_____

©South-Western Educational Publishing

Chapter 4 OUTLINE
Government and Global Business

GLOBAL FOCUS: U.S. DEPARTMENT OF AGRICULTURE PROMOTES THE FOOD EXPORTS

LESSON 4-1 POLITICS AND GLOBAL BUSINESS

TYPES OF POLITICAL SYSTEMS

DEMOCRACY

TOTALITARIANISM

MIXED SYSTEMS

POLITICAL RELATIONSHIPS IN BUSINESS

GLOBAL COMPANIES OPERATING IN HOST COUNTRIES

GLOBAL COMPANIES' RELATIONSHIPS WITH HOME COUNTRIES

LESSON FEATURES
GLOBAL BUSINESS EXAMPLE: THE VIEW FROM CHINA

REGIONAL PERSPECTIVE: HISTORY: TEOTIHUACAN

LESSON 4-2 HOW GOVERNMENT DISCOURAGES GLOBAL BUSINESS

GOVERNMENT ACTIVITIES INFLUENCE BUSINESS

LAWS THAT PROTECT WORKERS AND CONSUMERS

TRADE BARRIERS

Tariffs

Quotas

Boycotts

Licensing Requirements

POLITICAL RISKS IN INTERNATIONAL BUSINESS

TRADE SANCTIONS

EXPROPRIATION

ECONOMIC NATIONALISM

CIVIL UNREST OR WAR

INTERNATIONAL TAXES

CUSTOMS DUTY

SALES TAX

EXCISE TAX

PAYROLL-RELATED TAX

VALUE-ADDED TAX (VAT)

INCOME TAXES

©South-Western Educational Publishing

LESSON FEATURES

GLOBAL BUSINESS EXAMPLE: CONSUMER PROTECTION LAWS AROUND THE WORLD

GLOBAL BUSINESS EXAMPLE: POLITICAL RISKS AND PERSONAL DANGER

LESSON 4-3 HOW GOVERNMENT ENCOURAGES GLOBAL BUSINESS

ENCOURAGING INTERNATIONAL BUSINESS

FREE-TRADE ZONES

MOST FAVORED NATION

FREE-TRADE AGREEMENTS

COMMON MARKETS

GOVERNMENT PROTECTION FROM INTERNATIONAL RISK

TAX INCENTIVES

LESSON FEATURES
A QUESTION OF ETHICS: PAYING FOR SPECIAL FAVORS

E-COMMERCE IN ACTION: ONLINE EXPORTING ASSISTANCE

©South-Western Educational Publishing

Lesson 4-1
Politics and Global Business

LESSON QUIZ

Directions: For each of the following statements, if the statement is true, write a T on the answer line; if the statement is false, write an F on the answer line.

_____ 1. A democracy is a political system in which all citizens take part in making the rules that govern them.

_____ 2. Democratic societies do not usually have a market economy.

_____ 3. A totalitarian political system usually has a dictatorship in which the military makes all the decisions.

_____ 4. Most countries have either a pure democratic system or a pure totalitarian system; mixed systems are rare.

_____ 5. A multinational enterprise in a host country must operate within the host country's economic, social, and legal constraints.

_____ 6. Multinational companies usually do not benefit the citizens of the host country.

_____ 7. A multinational company needs to exhibit social responsibility in both its host countries and its home country.

Directions: For each of the following items, decide which choice best completes the statement. Write the letter that identifies your choice on the answer line.

_____ 8. Of the following characteristics, the one that is not typical of a democratic system is that
   A. individuals have the freedom to own and operate private businesses.
   B. individuals can build a small business into a very large business.
   C. the economy is usually a command economy.
   D. individuals may travel freely to other countries.

_____ 9. A political system in which one political party holds all the power and prohibits members of other parties from participating is a
   A. democracy.
   B. totalitarian system.
   C. exclusive system.
   D. none of these

_____ 10. A multinational enterprise is not acting with social responsibility if it
   A. installs anti-pollution controls more powerful than required by law.
   B. hires host-country citizens and provides training.
   C. introduces new products that support dominant religious beliefs of the host country.
   D. hires all employees from the home country labor force.

Activity 1 • Identifying Political Systems

Directions: Place a check mark in the appropriate column to indicate which kind of political system is most likely being described.

		Democracy	Totalitarian System	Mixed System
1.	Four companies operate television cable systems in this country but must follow extensive broadcasting regulations set by government.			
2.	Powerful generals in the army have overthrown the hereditary monarch and are now ruling the country.			
3.	The country has just held its first national elections and elected its leaders from several different political parties.			
4.	Individuals are permitted to open small roadside markets but may not build a canning factory.			
5.	The government owns and operates the train and bus system but private companies furnish electrical power.			

Activity 2 • Identifying Opportunities for Social Responsibility

Directions: A multinational enterprise is planning a new operation in a less-developed country. Its managers believe that the new operation will be more successful if the company acts in a socially responsible way in this country. Suggest ways the company can show social responsibility in each of the following areas.

6. Education: _____

_____

_____

_____

7. Employment: _____

_____

_____

_____

8. Environment: _____

_____

_____

_____

9. Technology: _____

_____

_____

_____

 ©South-Western Educational Publishing

Lesson 4-2
How Government Discourages Global Business

LESSON QUIZ

Directions: For each of the following statements, if the statement is true, write a T on the answer line; if the statement is false, write an F on the answer line.

_____ 1. An outbreak of civil war within a country is an example of political risk.

_____ 2. Value-added tax is added only when the final product is sold to the consumer.

_____ 3. Import quotas are used to help protect domestic companies from foreign competition.

_____ 4. Customs duties are often assessed to make imported products more expensive than similar products produced locally.

_____ 5. A foreign buyer who goes bankrupt before paying off his debt is an example of political risk.

_____ 6. Sales taxes are regressive taxes because people with a lower income pay a larger percentage of their income than do people with a higher income.

_____ 7. Personal income taxes are progressive taxes because they are usually set up so that the more one earns, the higher percentage of income taxes that person pays.

_____ 8. A double taxation avoidance treaty between two countries allows each country to tax the multinational corporation on the same earned income.

_____ 9. A tax holiday releases foreign investors from paying corporate income taxes.

_____10. Excise taxes are examples of payroll taxes.

Directions: For each of the following items, decide which choice best completes the statement. Write the letter that identifies your choice on the answer line.

_____11. Tariffs, quotas, and boycotts are examples of
   A. civil unrest.
   B. political unrest.
   C. trade barriers.
   D. none of these

_____12. Value-added and excise taxes are taxes on
   A. the sale of goods.
   B. corporate income.
   C. payroll.
   D. none of these

_____13. Protectionism policies such as tariffs and quotas are used because
   A. the government wants to make it harder for companies in other countries to compete with local companies.
   B. consumers need to be protected from inferior or hazardous products.
   C. the country needs additional revenue.
   D. none of these

Activity 1 • Analyzing Different Viewpoints about a Boycott

Different people have different points of view about specific government actions that affect international business. The Japanese government's trade policy bans the importation of rice.

Directions: Describe the viewpoint you think each of the following people would have about the ban on imported rice in Japan and explain why each person would have this viewpoint.

1. A Japanese rice farmer

   Viewpoint _____

   _____

   Explanation _____

   _____

2. A U.S. exporter of rice

   Viewpoint _____

   Explanation _____

   _____

3. A Japanese government trade official

   Viewpoint _____

   _____

   Explanation _____

   _____

4. A Japanese consumer of rice

   Viewpoint _____

   _____

   Explanation _____

   _____

   _____

5. A U.S. government official responsible for increasing U.S. exports of agricultural products

   Viewpoint _____

   _____

   Explanation _____

   _____

   _____

©South-Western Educational Publishing

Lesson 4-3
How Government Encourages Global Business

LESSON QUIZ

Directions: For each of the following statements, if the statement is true, write a T on the answer line; if the statement is false, write an F on the answer line.

_____ 1. The United States is the only country whose government provides export counseling.

_____ 2. Governments try to discourage other countries from investing and locating plants in their countries by using tax incentives.

_____ 3. A country with most favored nation status usually exports into the granting country at lower customs duty rates than other companies.

_____ 4. A free-trade agreement between two companies results in increased trade between the countries because barriers to trade are removed.

_____ 5. The main reason countries join together in a common market is to allow workers to move freely across borders.

_____ 6. If a U.S. exporter has export credit insurance from EXIM, its shipments are insured against damage or destruction caused by wars, revolutions, and civil disorders.

_____ 7. The more taxes there are on a business, the higher the price the business charges consumers for its products.

Directions: For each of the following items, decide which choice best completes the statement. Write the letter that identifies your choice on the answer line.

_____ 8. Governments encourage and promote its country's exports primarily because
A. exports create jobs and foster economic prosperity.
B. exports increase the country's international image and reputation.
C. exports increase government revenues by selling export insurance.
D. none of these

_____ 9. When two countries agree to eliminate duties and trade barriers on products traded between them, they have
A. free-trade zones.
B. most favored nation status.
C. a free trade-agreement.
D. all of these

_____10. When countries join together to eliminate duties and other trade barriers, allow companies to invest freely in each other's country, and allow workers to move freely across borders, they are said to have
A. free-trade zones.
B. most favored nation status.
C. a free trade-agreement.
D. a common market.

Activity 1 • Analyzing International Business Risks

Susan Thomas is the Vice President of International Business for the Major Machinery Company. Major Machinery is a U.S. multinational company with plants in Brazil, Indonesia, India, the United Kingdom, Mexico, Germany, Italy, and Japan. One of Ms. Thomas's responsibilities is to predict possible political risk that would negatively affect any of the company's overseas plants.

Directions: Answer the following questions.

1. How could Ms. Thomas predict political risk? What types of information could she collect to monitor potential political "trouble spots" around the world? What does she need to do to keep informed of actions of the U.S. government that might adversely affect her firm?

_____

_____

_____

_____

_____

_____

_____

_____

_____

_____

_____

_____

_____

_____

_____

_____

_____

_____

2. If the Major Machinery Company is planning to export to countries that have been identified as risky by Ms. Thomas, how could the company protect itself from loss?

_____

_____

_____

_____

_____

_____

Chapter 5 OUTLINE
Structures of International Business Organizations

GLOBAL FOCUS: MITSUBISHI: FROM TRADING COMPANY TO MULTINATIONAL CORPORATION

LESSON 5-1 METHODS OF BUSINESS OWNERSHIP

THE SOLE PROPRIETORSHIP

ADVANTAGES OF A SOLE PROPRIETORSHIP

Ease of Starting

Freedom to Make Business Decisions

Owner Keeps All Profits

Pride of Ownership

DISADVANTAGES OF A SOLE PROPRIETORSHIP

Limited Sources of Funds

Long Hours and Hard Work

Unlimited Risks

Limited Life of the business

PARTNERSHIP

ADVANTAGES OF A PARTNERSHIP

Ease of Creation

Additional Sources of Funds

Availability of Different Talents

DISADVANTAGES OF A PARTNERSHIP

 ©South-Western Educational Publishing

Partners Are Liable

Profits Are Shared among Several Owners

Potential for Disagreement among Owners

Business Can Dissolve Suddenly

CORPORATION

ADVANTAGES OF A CORPORATION

More Sources of Funds

Fixed Financial Liability of Owners

Specialized Management

Unlimited Life of the Company

DISADVANTAGES OF A CORPORATION

Difficult Creation Process

Owners Have Limited Control

Double Taxation

LESSON FEATURE
GLOBAL BUSINESS EXAMPLE: HOW DO YOU SPELL INC.?

LESSON 5-2 OPERATIONS OF GLOBAL BUSINESSES

OTHER FORMS OF BUSINESS ORGANIZATION

MULTINATIONAL COMPANIES

MULTINATIONAL COMPANIES IN OPERATION

CHARACTERISTICS OF MULTINATIONAL COMPANIES

 ©South-Western Educational Publishing

World-Wide Market View

Standardized Product

Culturally-Sensitive Hiring

International and Local Perspective

CONCERNS ABOUT MULTINATIONAL COMPANIES

LESSON FEATURES
COMMUNICATION ACROSS BORDERS: KOMATSU ABANDONS JAPANESE FOR ENGLISH

GLOBAL BUSINESS EXAMPLE: BUSINESSES EXPAND TO MALAYSIA

REGIONAL PERSPECTIVE: HISTORY: AUSTRALIA'S IMPORTING OF CONVICTS

LESSON 5-3 STARTING GLOBAL BUSINESS ACTIVITIES

LOW-RISK METHODS FOR GETTING INVOLVED IN INTERNATIONAL BUSINESS

INDIRECT EXPORTING

DIRECT EXPORTING

MANAGEMENT CONTRACTING

LICENSING

FRANCHISING

HIGHER-RISK METHODS FOR GETTING INVOLVED IN INTERNATIONAL BUSINESS

JOINT VENTURES

FOREIGN DIRECT INVESTMENT

LESSON FEATURES
A QUESTION OF ETHICS: STEALING SECRETS BY FOREIGN PARTNERS

GLOBAL BUSINESS EXAMPLE: CEREAL PARTNERS WORLDWIDE

 ©South-Western Educational Publishing

Lesson 5-1
Methods of Business Ownership

LESSON QUIZ

Directions: For each of the following statements, if the statement is true, write a T on the answer line; if the statement is false, write an F on the answer line.

_____ 1. Only a few businesses in the United States are organized as sole proprietorships.

_____ 2. Partners have unlimited liability and may be personally responsible for the debts of their business.

_____ 3. If one partner buys expensive equipment for the partnership without consulting the other partner, only that partner is liable for the cost of the equipment.

_____ 4. Forming a business in partnership with another person has the advantage of sharing resources and skills but has the disadvantage of possible disagreements over different opinions on how to run the business.

_____ 5. Compared to a partnership, a corporation is fairly easy to create.

_____ 6. One way to raise money to operate a corporation is to sell portions of ownership to the public.

_____ 7. *Limited liability* means that stockholders can lose their investment if the corporation fails.

_____ 8. The earnings of a corporation may be taxed twice.

Directions: For each of the following items, decide which choice best completes the statement. Write the letter that identifies your choice on the answer line.

_____ 9. *Double taxation* means that
   A. each partner in a partnership pays income tax on the earnings of the business.
   B. an owner of a sole proprietorship pays personal income tax on the earnings of the business.
   C. both a corporation and its stockholders pay income taxes on earnings of the corporation.
   D. none of these

_____ 10. *Unlimited liability* means that
   A. if a sole proprietorship fails, the business's creditors may force the owner to sell personal property, such as a house and car, to pay the amounts owed.
   B. each partner in a partnership may independently make decisions affecting the partnership.
   C. all stockholders who own shares of a corporation vote on who will manage the corporation.
   D. none of these

_____ 11. A disadvantage of the corporate form of business ownership is that
   A. owners earn a return on the money they have invested in the form of dividends.
   B. stockholders in large corporations have little direct control over how the company is managed.
   C. stockholders are not personally liable for the debts of the corporation except to the extent of their investment.
   D. none of these

Activity 1 • Identifying Advantages and Disadvantages of Sole Proprietorships, Partnerships, and Corporations

Directions: For each item in the following list, decide if it is an advantage or disadvantage of a sole proprietorship, partnership, or corporation. In the appropriate column, enter A if it is an advantage or D if it is a disadvantage. (Some items may be an advantage or a disadvantage of more than one form of business organization.)

		Sole Proprietorship	Partnership	Corporation
1.	Ease of starting			
2.	Availability of different talents			
3.	Owner keeps all profits			
4.	Unlimited liability			
5.	A difficult creation process			
6.	Limited sources of funds			
7.	Unlimited life of the company			
8.	Potential disagreement among owners			
9.	Double taxation of earnings			
10.	Business can dissolve suddenly			
11.	Availability of specialized management			
12.	Limited liability			

Activity 2 • Graphing Business Organization Data

Directions: Prepare a bar graph that presents the number of sole proprietorships, partnerships, and corporations for the central region, as identified in the following table.

Type of Business Ownership	Central Region
Sole proprietorships	57,000
Partnerships	11,000
Corporations	28,500

TYPES OF BUSINESS IN THE CENTRAL REGION

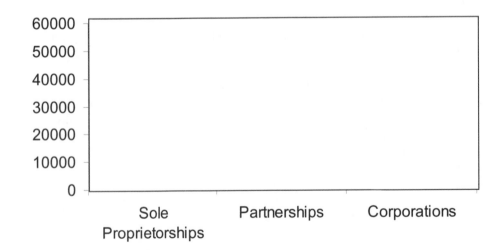

Lesson 5-2
Operations of Global Businesses

LESSON QUIZ

Directions: For each of the following statements, if the statement is true, write a T on the answer line; if the statement is false, write an F on the answer line.

_____ 1. Municipal corporations do not usually engage in international business activities.

_____ 2. Nonprofit corporations provide a service but do not try to make a profit.

_____ 3. Like nonprofit corporations, cooperatives do not make profits.

_____ 4. A cooperative is an example of a government-owned corporation.

_____ 5. Multinational companies are commonly called monopolies.

_____ 6. Multinational companies only pay taxes to the government in their home countries.

_____ 7. A multinational company is said to have a world-wide market view because it views the entire world as a potential customer.

_____ 8. Although there is a risk of a multinational company's influencing politics in a host country, the company may also provide many benefits such as more jobs, products, and even improvements to the infrastructure of the country.

Directions: For each of the following items, decide which choice best completes the statement. Write the letter that identifies your choice on the answer line.

_____ 9. Business organizations that are formed to provide services without regard to making a profit are
   A. municipal corporations and nonprofit corporations.
   B. nonprofit corporations and cooperatives.
   C. cooperatives and multinational corporations.
   D. none of these

_____ 10. An example of a cooperative is a
   A. credit union.
   B. hospital.
   C. private college.
   D. none of these

_____ 11. Of the following statements, the one that does not describe a multinational company is that
   A. it maintains both an international and local perspective.
   B. a country may become too dependent on it.
   C. its strength is that it offers a different product in each market.
   D. none of these

_____ 12. Many people believe that multinational companies need to be regulated and controlled because
   A. they make too much money.
   B. they may dominate a country's economy and control the political situation.
   C. they do not employ citizens of the host countries to a large enough extent.
   D. none of these

Activity 1 • Analyzing News about Multinational Companies

Directions: Locate a recent newspaper or magazine article about a company that does business in more than one country. Use this article to provide the following information and answer the following questions.

Title of article _____

Author _____

Source of article _____

Date _____

1. How would you rate the reliability of the source of this article? Explain your reasons. _____

_____

_____

2. What is the name of the company and what products or services does the company sell? _____

_____

_____

_____

3. In what nations does the company do business? _____

_____

_____

4. Based on the article and your knowledge of international business, what actions were required by the company to do business in other countries? _____

_____

_____

_____

_____

5. How is the company viewed in the countries in which it does business? Cite evidence from the article to support your view. _____

_____

_____

_____

_____

_____

6. What additional information would you like to have about this company or its international business activities? _____

_____

_____

©South-Western Educational Publishing

Lesson 5-3
Starting Global Business Activities

LESSON QUIZ

Directions: For each of the following statements, if the statement is true, write a T on the answer line; if the statement is false, write an F on the answer line.

_____ 1. The simplest, lowest-risk method of getting involved in international business is to form a joint venture with a company in another country.

_____ 2. Franchising is also known as indirect exporting.

_____ 3. One reason direct exporting is a relatively low-risk method of getting involved in international business is because the exporting company does not have an extensive investment in another country.

_____ 4. Contract manufacturing can be a form of international business if the manufacturer produces products for a company located in another country.

_____ 5. A joint venture is an agreement between two or more companies to share a business project.

_____ 6. Real estate purchased in another country is called foreign direct investment.

Directions: For each of the following items, decide which choice best completes the statement. Write the letter that identifies your choice on the answer line.

_____ 7. Of the following methods for getting involved in international business, the one with the lowest risk is
A. joint venture.
B. licensing.
C. management contracting.
D. foreign direct investment.

_____ 8. Of the following methods for getting involved in international business, the one with the highest risk is
A. joint venture.
B. licensing.
C. management contracting.
D. foreign direct investment.

_____ 9. An example of licensing is when
A. a business in France contracts to produce shirts with the image of an American band.
B. a company in Brazil contracts to open a Kentucky Fried Chicken restaurant.
C. a company in New Zealand produces tires for a tractor manufacturer in Japan.
D. all of these

_____ 10. Of the following statements, the one that does not describe a joint venture is
A. two or more companies agree to share a business project.
B. they are especially popular for manufacturing projects because plants and facilities and resources can be shared.
C. all participating companies share the risks and benefits equally.
D. the higher risk can lead to greater profits.

Activity 1 • Identifying Methods for Getting Involved in International Business

Directions: Match the following methods of conducting international business with the descriptions below. Some items will be used more than once.

A. wholly-owned subsidiary

B. joint venture

C. licensing

D. direct exporting

E. foreign direct investment

F. franchising

G. management contracting

H. indirect exporting

_____ 1. A company sells supervisory seminars to train computer managers in developing countries.

_____ 2. A motor vehicle manufacturer creates a new department within the company to sell its cars and trucks in other countries.

_____ 3. A medical supply company from Canada and a hospital in Turkey unite to create a new business.

_____ 4. The Continental Wire Company of Chile buys real estate in New Zealand for future use as a factory site.

_____ 5. A company that produces animated television programs sells the rights to use its characters on shirts and other items throughout the world.

_____ 6. Brown Electronics has its company representatives visit countries in northern Africa to sell its products.

_____ 7. A small producer of clothing in England is contacted by a buying agent from Brazil.

_____ 8. A French restaurant company contracts to allow its name and menu items to be used in other countries.

_____ 9. A Japanese company buys and operates a food producer based in the United States.

_____10. A health-care company from the United States works to help set up clinics in other countries.

Activity 2 • Analyzing Methods for Getting Involved in International Business

Directions: Provide short answers for the following questions.

11. What is the simplest method of getting involved in international business? _____

12. What is the relationship between risk and profit? _____

_____

13. What is the main difference between indirect and direct exporting? _____

_____

_____

14. What is a company selling in a management contract situation? _____

_____

15. What are some popular intangible properties that have potential for international licensing today? _____

_____

16. Other than fast-food companies, what are some businesses in your community that are probably franchises? _____

_____

 ©South-Western Educational Publishing

Chapter 6 OUTLINE
Importing, Exporting, and Trade Relations

GLOBAL FOCUS: THE SCOOP ON ICE CREAM EXPORTS

LESSON 6-1 IMPORTING PROCEDURES

THE IMPORTANCE OF IMPORTING

PRODUCT DEMAND

LOWER COSTS

PRODUCTION INPUTS

IMPORTING ACTIVITIES

STEP ONE: DETERMINE DEMAND

STEP TWO: CONTACT SUPPLIERS

STEP THREE: FINALIZE PURCHASE

STEP FOUR: RECEIVE GOODS

IMPORT ASSISTANCE

LESSON FEATURES
GLOBAL BUSINESS EXAMPLE: AN IMPORTING ERROR

REGIONAL PERSPECTIVE: HISTORY: THE GREAT WALL OF CHINA

LESSON 6-2 EXPORTING PROCEDURES

THE EXPORTING PROCESS

STEP ONE: FIND POTENTIAL CUSTOMERS

STEP TWO: MEET THE NEEDS OF CUSTOMERS

STEP THREE: AGREE ON SALES TERMS

STEP FOUR: PROVIDE PRODUCTS OR SERVICES

STEP FIVE: COMPLETE THE TRANSACTION

OTHER EXPORTING ISSUES

AVOID EXPORTING HURDLES

EXPORTING SERVICES

LESSON FEATURES
E-COMMERCE IN ACTION: E-TAILING AND LOWER BARRIERS TO ENTRY

GLOBAL BUSINESS EXAMPLE: EXPORTING CULTURE

LESSON 6-3 IMPORTANCE OF TRADE RELATIONS

THE ECONOMIC EFFECT OF FOREIGN TRADE

TRADE AGREEMENTS

THE WORLD TRADE ORGANIZATION

ECONOMIC COMMUNITIES

BARTER AGREEMENTS

FREE-TRADE ZONES

LESSON FEATURE
GLOBAL BUSINESS EXAMPLE: EUROPEAN UNION

LESSON 6-4 THE NATURE OF COMPETITION

INTERNATIONAL BUSINESS COMPETITION

FACTORS AFFECTING COMPETITION

Number of Companies

Business Costs

Product Differences

BENEFITS AND CONCERNS OF COMPETITION

TYPES OF COMPETITIVE SITUATIONS

PURE COMPETITION

MONOPOLISTIC COMPETITION

OLIGOPOLY

MONOPOLY

LESSON FEATURE
COMMUNICATION ACROSS BORDERS: UNDERSTANDING ASIAN NAMES

 ©South-Western Educational Publishing

Lesson 6-1
Importing Procedures

LESSON QUIZ

Directions: For each of the following statements, if the statement is true, write a T on the answer line; if the statement is false, write an F on the answer line.

_____ 1. An item you buy that is made in another country is an example of an import.

_____ 2. Customs officials sell imported products in government-owned stores.

_____ 3. Some goods have to be imported because they are only available from foreign sources.

_____ 4. An importing business is involved in international business when it buys goods from other countries and then sells them in its own country.

_____ 5. The risk involved in importing is increased if you do not first determine whether there is any demand for the product you plan to import.

_____ 6. It is usually easy to locate foreign suppliers who can provide the goods you want to import, when you need them.

_____ 7. Customs duties are always based on the value of the goods, not quantity or weight.

Directions: For each of the following items, decide which choice best completes the statement. Write the letter that identifies your choice on the answer line.

_____ 8. Importing is important because of the following two reasons
  A. customers want the product and it is cheaper from another country.
  B. your country has a competitive advantage and home-country products are more expensive.
  C. availability of parts for manufacturing and customs duties.
  D. none of these

_____ 9. A purchase agreement should include all of the following details except
  A. who will pay for shipping.
  B. the amount of customs duty.
  C. how the payment will be made.
  D. when the items will be delivered.

_____ 10. Of the following business transactions, the only one that describes an importing activity is
  A. a wholesaler in Brazil packs goods for shipment to Liberia.
  B. a retailer in Sweden receives goods from Mexico to sell in a chain of stores.
  C. a restaurant food supplier in Japan ships sushi ingredients to a restaurant in Turkey.
  D. none of these

Activity 1 • Analyzing the Importance of Importing Activities

Directions: For each of the following four steps of importing, describe why each step is important.

1. Step One: Determine Demand _____

_____

_____

_____

_____

2. Step Two: Contact Suppliers _____

_____

_____

_____

_____

3. Step Three: Finalize Purchase _____

_____

_____

_____

_____

4. Step Four: Receive Goods _____

_____

_____

_____

_____

Activity 2 • Comparing Importing and Domestic Business Activities

Directions: In the space below, write a paragraph that compares the steps in the importing process with domestic business practices.

5. _____

_____

_____

_____

_____

_____

_____

_____

_____

_____

 ©South-Western Educational Publishing

Lesson 6-2
Exporting Procedures

LESSON QUIZ

Directions: For each of the following statements, if the statement is true, write a T on the answer line; if the statement is false, write an F on the answer line.

_____ 1. Indirect exporting involves a company's export department selling to manufacturers in another country.

_____ 2. When food products are exported, they can usually be standardized for most countries.

_____ 3. When sales terms are described as *cost and freight (C&F)*, this means that all costs of the goods, shipping, and insurance are included in the price.

_____ 4. When imported products are in high demand or are extremely perishable, water transport by ship is usually the best method of transportation.

_____ 5. A freight forwarder arranges the shipping of goods to customers in other countries.

_____ 6. The purpose of a bill of lading is to identify the country in which the goods were produced.

_____ 7. Many U.S. companies successfully export products to other companies, but exports of services are very rare.

Directions: For each of the following items, decide which choice best completes the statement. Write the letter that identifies your choice on the answer line.

_____ 8. A U.S. company exported kitchen appliances to Italy without changing the appliances. Italians did not buy the appliances because they would not work with the way Italian electricity current is supplied to households. The step in the exporting process the exporter did not properly complete is
   A. to agree on sales terms.
   B. to provide products or services.
   C. to meet the needs of customers.
   D. to complete the transaction.

_____ 9. A certificate of origin is a document used in exporting that
   A. may be used to determine the amount of import tax.
   B. states the agreement between the importer and the transportation company.
   C. serves as a receipt for the shipment of goods.
   D. none of these

_____ 10. When goods are exported to another company
   A. the quickest method of shipment should be used.
   B. the least expensive method of shipment should be used.
   C. the method of shipment varies depending on the product and other factors.
   D. none of these

_____ 11. Products that do not usually require much modification for foreign customers include
   A. laundry detergent.
   B. skin care products.
   C. clothing.
   D. none of these

Activity 1 • Identifying Importing-Exporting Activities

Directions: For each of the following situations, if the country printed in bold type is importing, write an I on the answer line; if the country is exporting, write an E on the answer line.

_____ 1. A **Canadian** company buys parts from a company in another country for use in making computers.

_____ 2. An Egyptian buying agent arranges for the purchase of clothing made in **Ecuador**.

_____ 3. A management company from **Spain** is paid a fee to set up computer systems in Australia.

_____ 4. A **Greek** manufacturing company purchases raw materials from Kenya.

_____ 5. A **Swedish** fast-food company allows companies in Norway to use its name and business processes.

_____ 6. A company in **Pakistan** sells its shirts to a company in England.

_____ 7. A **U.S.** automobile manufacturer buys parts from Mexico.

_____ 8. A computer store in **Iran** sells hardware manufactured in England.

_____ 9. A consumer in Pakistan buys athletic shoes that were made in **Japan**.

_____10. A jewelry maker in **France** buys diamonds from South Africa.

Activity 2 • Identifying the Steps of the Exporting Process

Directions: The steps of the exporting process are listed below, out of order. Rewrite the steps in the appropriate order. Then answer the question that follows.

• Agree on sales terms
• Provide products or services
• Complete the transaction
• Find potential customers
• Meet the needs of customers

11. Step 1. _____

12. Step 2. _____

13. Step 3. _____

14. Step 4. _____

15. Step 5. _____

16. Briefly describe how the exporting process differs from the importing process.

_____

_____

_____

_____

_____

_____

 ©South-Western Educational Publishing

Lesson 6-3
Importance of Trade Relations

LESSON QUIZ

Directions: For each of the following statements, if the statement is true, write a T on the answer line; if the statement is false, write an F on the answer line.

_____ 1. When exports are greater than imports there is a favorable balance of trade.

_____ 2. An unfavorable balance of payments occurs when a nation receives more money from international trade in one year than it pays out.

_____ 3. A trade deficit occurs when imports are greater than exports.

_____ 4. A country's balance of payments is a better measure of international business then the balance of trade because it includes more exchanges with foreign sources.

_____ 5. Direct barter occurs when a company pays directly for imported goods.

_____ 6. Countertrade is a method of barter that never includes cash payments.

_____ 7. Items bought at a free-trade zone of an airport and then taken into the country are subject to the customs duties of that country.

Directions: For each of the following items, decide which choice best completes the statement. Write the letter that identifies your choice on the answer line.

_____ 8. A country with exports of $6 million and imports of $10 million has a
  A. trade surplus.
  B. trade deficit.
  C. favorable balance of payments.
  D. unfavorable balance of payments.

_____ 9. A country with exports of $6 million and other cash coming into the country of $3 million and imports of $5 million and other cash going out of the country of $3 million has a
  A. trade surplus.
  B. trade deficit.
  C. favorable balance of payments.
  D. unfavorable balance of payments.

_____ 10. Money given as foreign aid to another country
  A. decreases the balance of payments of the country making the payment.
  B. increases the balance of payments of the country making the payment.
  C. has a negative effect on the trade deficit.
  D. none of these

_____ 11. Countertrade is
  A. a method of direct barter.
  B. a method of avoiding payments in a currency with limited value.
  C. not a barter method.
  D. none of these

Activity 1 • Identifying Methods for Getting Involved in International Business

Directions: For each of the following situations, determine if a favorable or unfavorable balance of payments exists and calculate the amount.

	Country	Total Inflows (in millions)	Total Outflows (in millions)	Favorable or Unfavorable	Amount (in millions)
1.	Bolivia	$B2,090	$B2,079		
2.	Libya	LD1,576	LD1,568		
3.	New Zealand	NZ$16,150	NZ$15,980		
4.	Romania	L358,900	L525,400		
5.	Thailand	B838,755	B513,000		

Activity 2 • Analyzing Reasons for International Transactions

Directions: Provide short answers to answer the following questions.

6. Why would a government provide incentives for tourists to visit a country? _____

_____

_____

_____

7. Why does the U.S. government have several agencies that provide import and export information and advice to companies? _____

_____

_____

_____

8. Why would a country give another country financial assistance but require that capital projects using that money be contracted with the granting country? _____

_____

_____

9. Why would a country encourage foreign investors? _____

_____

_____

_____

 ©South-Western Educational Publishing

Lesson 6-4
The Nature of Competition

LESSON QUIZ

Directions: For each of the following statements, if the statement is true, write a T on the answer line; if the statement is false, write an F on the answer line.

_____ 1. The company with the best product is the most successful in the market.

_____ 2. Competition will usually improve the economic situation and living conditions of a nation.

_____ 3. Governments often place legal limits on the power of companies so that one dominant company cannot control a geographic area or portion of an economy.

_____ 4. An industry is a group of companies in the same type of business.

_____ 5. The candy bar industry is an example of pure competition.

_____ 6. Monopolistic competition occurs when a few large companies control an industry.

_____ 7. It is unusual for a monopoly to occur without the influence of government or other businesses.

Directions: For each of the following items, decide which choice best completes the statement. Write the letter that identifies your choice on the answer line.

_____ 8. A company can have a competitive advantage if it
A. produces a comparable product at the same cost as others in the market.
B. builds the best reputation for quality of all companies in the market.
C. has about the same manufacturing costs as other companies in the market.
D. none of these

_____ 9. The major factors that affect the degree of competition are
A. number of companies, amount of advertising, and number of factories.
B. number of companies, size of companies, and type of product.
C. number of companies, business costs, and product differences.
D. none of these

_____ 10. An industry that has a few large companies that control it is
A. pure competition.
B. monopolistic competition.
C. an oligopoly.
D. a monopoly.

_____ 11. An industry that has many companies offering the same basic product, but with some slight differences is
A. pure competition.
B. monopolistic competition.
C. an oligopoly.
D. a monopoly.

Activity 1 • Examining Competitive Situations

Directions: Find examples of two different types of market situations. In the area below, record (a) the product or service, (b) the type of competitive situation, and (c) names of a few companies in that industry. Do not use the same examples given in the textbook. The following information can help you analyze different industries.

Pure Competition
- many sellers
- same product

Monopolistic Competition
- many sellers
- slightly different product

Oligopoly
- few sellers
- slightly different product

Monopoly
- one seller
- usually government regulated

	(a) Product or Service	(b) Type of Competitive Situation	(c) Companies in the Industry
1.			
2.			

Activity 2 • Analyzing Competitive Advantage

Directions: Competitive advantage in an industry can be the result of one or several factors, including quality, speed, price, service, availability, advertising, or other factors. For this activity, list several products that you buy and describe the competitive advantage of that product that persuades you to buy it. List the brand name or company name of the product, or both if you know them both.

	Brand Name/ Company Name	(b) Competitive Advantage
3.		
4.		
5.		
6.		
7.		
8.		

©South-Western Educational Publishing

Chapter 7 OUTLINE
Foreign Exchange and International Finance

GLOBAL FOCUS: AN UNEXPECTED CURRENCY FOR UKRAINE

LESSON 7-1 MONEY SYSTEMS AROUND THE WORLD

MONEY AND CURRENCY SYSTEMS

WHAT IS MONEY?

Acceptability

Scarcity

Durability

Divisibility

Portability

WHY IS MONEY USED?

Medium of Exchange

Measure of Value

Store of Value

FOREIGN EXCHANGE

BALANCE OF PAYMENTS

ECONOMIC CONDITIONS

Money Supply and Demand

Risk

Inflation

POLITICAL STABILITY

LESSON FEATURE
A QUESTION OF ETHICS: PRINTING ADDITIONAL CURRENCY

LESSON 7-2 FOREIGN EXCHANGE AND CURRENCY CONTROLS

FOREIGN EXCHANGE ACTIVITIES

CHANGING EXCHANGE RATES

THE FOREIGN EXCHANGE MARKET

FOREIGN EXCHANGE CONTROLS

INTERNATIONAL FINANCIAL AGENCIES

THE WORLD BANK

THE INTERNATIONAL MONETARY FUND (IMF)

Analyze Economic Situations

Suggest Economic Policies

Provide Loans

LESSON FEATURES
GLOBAL BUSINESS EXAMPLE: FOREIGN EXCHANGE AND TOURISM

GLOBAL BUSINESS EXAMPLE: CALCULATING FOREIGN EXCHANGE

GLOBAL BUSINESS EXAMPLE: THE ECONOMIC AND TRADE PROBLEMS OF GHANA

©South-Western Educational Publishing

LESSON 7-3 CURRENCY TRANSACTIONS BETWEEN NATIONS

INTERNATIONAL FINANCIAL TRANSACTIONS

FOREIGN TRADE PAYMENT METHODS

Cash in Advance

Letter of Credit

Sale on Account

SOURCES OF INTERNATIONAL FINANCING

Short-term Financing

Long-term Financing

OTHER PAYMENT METHODS AND FINANCIAL DOCUMENTS

Promissory Note

Bill of Exchange

Electronic Funds

Commercial Invoice

Insurance Certificate

LESSON FEATURES
E-COMMERCE IN ACTION: EUROPEAN E-CASH

REGIONAL PERSPECTIVE: HISTORY: VIETNAM: A NATION DIVIDED

 ©South-Western Educational Publishing

Lesson 7-1
Money Systems Around the World

LESSON QUIZ

Directions: For each of the following statements, if the statement is true, write a T on the answer line; if the statement is false, write an F on the answer line.

_____ 1. The only items used as money are coins and currency issued by a government.

_____ 2. Money is a medium of exchange only when it is exchanged for another currency.

_____ 3. An exchange rate is the amount of a currency of one country that can be traded for one unit of the currency of another country.

_____ 4. Barter usually makes it easier to compare the value of objects than money does.

_____ 5. When a country has a favorable balance of payments, the value of its currency is usually constant or rising.

_____ 6. As prices rise, lenders usually charge a lower interest rate on loans.

Directions: For each of the following items, decide which choice best completes the statement. Write the letter that identifies your choice on the answer line.

_____ 7. Shells were used as money once but would not work well as money today because
　　A. it would be difficult to persuade anyone to accept them as money.
　　B. they are not scarce.
　　C. they are fragile.
　　D. all of these

_____ 8. The exchange rate for a stable country
　　A. remains the same unless there is a political change.
　　B. changes somewhat from day to day.
　　C. is always based on the U.S. dollar.
　　D. none of these

_____ 9. The exchange rate for a country's currency will usually remain constant or increase if
　　A. the supply of currency increases but the demand does not.
　　B. inflation increases.
　　C. the balance of payments is favorable.
　　D. all of these

_____ 10. Of the following situations, the one that does not usually cause an increased interest rate is
　　A. political uncertainty.
　　B. when people are saving more and borrowing less.
　　C. when inflation is increasing.
　　D. none of these

Activity 1 • Identifying Functions of Money

Directions: For each of the following activities, decide whether the situation is an example of money as a medium of exchange, a measure of value, or a store of value. Place a check mark in the appropriate column to indicate your answer.

		Medium of Exchange	Measure of Value	Store of Value
1.	The exchange rate for U.S. dollars to Canadian dollars is 1.21.	~~✓~~	✓	
2.	A company in Europe must pay for imported goods with Mexican pesos.	✓		
3.	A student is saving £50 a month to help pay for college expenses.			✓
4.	A multinational company receives payment for the sale of goods and converts the funds into the currency of its home country.	✓	~~✓~~	
5.	Food for a week for a family of four in France costs Fr230 in one city and Fr267 in another city.		✓	
6.	An engineer makes a higher salary than an administrative assistant at the same company.	~~✓~~	✓	
7.	A shopper goes to three stores to compare prices on computer printers.		✓	
8.	A pair of a certain brand of jeans costs three times as much in a country where this kind of clothing is very scarce.		✓	

Activity 2 • Analyzing Factors Affecting Foreign Exchange

Directions: For each of the following international activities, indicate whether the value of the country's currency would increase or decrease by putting a check mark in the appropriate column. If you cannot determine the effect the activity would have on the currency, put a check mark in the last column.

		Increase	Decrease	Not Able to Determine
9.	A nation imports more than it exports.			
10.	Interest rates in a country rise.			
11.	A new president is elected in a country.			
12.	A nation's inflation rate drops.			
13.	The exports for a country increase as a result of technology.			
14.	The military seizes control of the government and takes over major industries.			
15.	New tourist attractions and international publicity increase international tourism by over one million people.			

©South-Western Educational Publishing

Lesson 7-2
Foreign Exchange and Currency Controls

LESSON QUIZ

Directions: For each of the following statements, if the statement is true, write a T on the answer line; if the statement is false, write an F on the answer line.

_____ 1. A soft currency is a monetary unit that is not easily exchanged for currencies of other countries.

_____ 2. Exchange controls usually allow the value of a country's currency to change based on supply and demand.

_____ 3. Usually when a country experiences high foreign demand for its products the demand results in a strong currency for the country because its manufacturers want to be paid in their own currency.

_____ 4. A company in one country buys a currency future to protect against an increase in that foreign currency's exchange rate sometime in the future.

_____ 5. An example of an exchange control is when a company limits the amount of its currency that tourists may take out of the country.

_____ 6. The primary goal of the World Bank is to maintain an orderly system of world trade and exchange rates.

_____ 7. A country's currency usually declines in value when the country's debt increases significantly.

Directions: For each of the following items, decide which choice best completes the statement. Write the letter that identifies your choice on the answer line.

_____ 8. A monetary unit that is freely converted into other currencies is
   A. a soft currency.
   B. a hard currency.
   C. an exchange control.
   D. none of these.

_____ 9. A system in which currency values are based on supply and demand is
   A. a foreign exchange market.
   B. a currency future.
   C. an exchange control.
   D. none of these

_____10. A currency future is
   A. an exchange rate.
   B. an exchange control.
   C. a contract.
   D. none of these

_____11. The International Monetary Fund (IMF)
   A. determines exchange rates.
   B. is a part of the foreign exchange market.
   C. provides capital and technical assistance to private businesses in nations with limited resources.
   D. helps maintain an orderly system of world trade and exchange rates.

Activity 1 • Applying Foreign Exchange Rates

Directions: Based on the following foreign exchange rate information, answer the questions below.

Currency	Value in U.S. Dollars	Units per U.S. Dollar
British pound(£)	$1.51	.66£
Canadian dollar	.73	1.37 Canadian dollars
German Deutsche Mark (DM)	.61	1.64 DM
Indian rupee	.032	31.25 rupees
Mexican peso	.30	3.33 pesos
South African rand	.27	3.70 rands

1. What would be the cost in U.S. dollars for a hotel room in Canada that costs 109 Canadian dollars?

   _____

2. If you purchased a camera for 234 deutsche marks, what would be the price in U.S. dollars?

   _____

3. While traveling in India, you purchase a hat costing $15 U.S. How many rupees would that be?

   _____

4. How many U.S. dollars would you need to buy a shirt that costs 70 pesos in Mexico?

   _____

5. You plan to take $450 U.S. on a trip to England. How many British pounds is this?

   _____

Part 2 • Graphing Foreign Exchange Rates

Directions: Select a currency from another country. Using information from a newspaper, graph the changing value of a U.S. dollar for several weeks. On the vertical axis, list the range of values for the foreign currency units per one U.S. dollar. Along the bottom, list the dates for your data points.

The Changing Value of the U.S. Dollar Compared to the _____

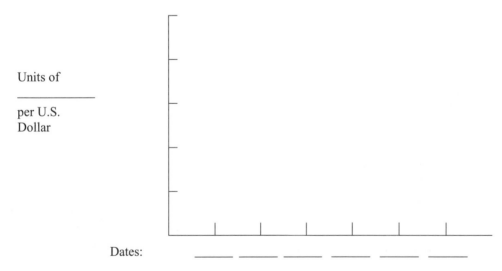

Units of

_____

per U.S.
Dollar

Dates: _____ _____ _____ _____ _____ _____

 ©South-Western Educational Publishing

Lesson 7-3
Currency Transactions Between Nations

LESSON QUIZ

Directions: For each of the following statements, if the statement is true, write a T on the answer line; if the statement is false, write an F on the answer line.

_____ 1. Accounts receivable are amounts owed by customers to a company that sells on credit.

_____ 2. Credit terms of 1/15, n/30 mean that a 15% discount may be taken on the amount due if paid before the normal 30 days.

_____ 3. A company has accounts receivable when it purchases items on account.

_____ 4. Trade credit is a method of short-term financing.

_____ 5. Long-term financing methods are often used for capital projects.

_____ 6. A bond represents ownership in a company.

_____ 7. A commercial invoice is a written order by an exporter to an importer to make payment, usually to a bank or other financial institution.

Directions: For each of the following items, decide which choice best completes the statement. Write the letter that identifies your choice on the answer line.

_____ 8. A document that states a promise to pay a set amount by a certain date is
   A. a letter of credit.
   B. an account payable.
   C. a bill of exchange.
   D. a promissory note.

_____ 9. Methods of short-term financing include
   A. trade credit and business loans.
   B. accounts payable, accounts receivable, and bonds.
   C. trade credit, bonds, and bills of exchange.
   D. accounts payable and accounts receivable.

_____ 10. A document prepared by an exporter that includes details about the buyer, seller, merchandise, prices, shipping method, date of shipment, and terms of payment is
   A. a promissory note.
   B. a bill of exchange.
   C. a commercial invoice.
   D. none of these

_____ 11. All of the following are examples of capital projects except
   A. installing a new computer and network system.
   B. buying a 6-month supply of packaging materials to take advantage of a 10% discount.
   C. buying ships to handle your own overseas transportation of goods.
   D. buying a company that competes with your own company.

Activity 1 • Analyzing International Financial Activities

Directions: For each of the following international business situations, select from the list the financial term that would be most appropriate. Write the letter that identifies the term on the answer line. (Note: Some terms may be used more than once.)

A. account receivable   **E.** commercial invoice

B. account payable   **F.** electronic funds transfer

C. bill of exchange   **G.** letter of credit

D. bond   **H.** promissory note

_____ 1. The need for a payment for foreign goods to arrive immediately.

_____ 2. Collins Imports wants to confirm its intention to pay for a purchase by a certain date.

_____ 3. An amount owed to a supplier.

_____ 4. Schmidt Food Products needs to borrow money that it will repay over the next 15 years.

_____ 5. Khan Exporting, Inc. has to inform an importer to make payment.

_____ 6. An exporter wants guaranteed payment for goods before shipping them.

_____ 7. Warsaw Electronics issues a document that confirms the amount of payment due with interest by a certain date.

_____ 8. For a manufacturer, the amount owed by an exporting company.

_____ 9. Joshua Manufacturing needs to deposit money by the end of the business day in a foreign bank.

_____10. Boston Exporting prepares a document that provides a detailed description of merchandise and the terms of a sale.

Activity 2 • Identifying Short-Term and Long-Term Financing

Directions: For each of the following statements, if the statement describes short-term financing, write an S on the answer line; if the statement describes long-term financing, write an L on the answer line. If the activity is not a financing activity, write an N on the answer line.

_____11. A company buys office supplies on account.

_____12. A company issues 10-year, 12% bonds to finance a new factory.

_____13. A company signs a promissory note due in 6 months for funds to buy seasonal merchandise.

_____14. A company takes out a 30-year mortgage on a new office building.

_____15. A company pays for a purchase of supplies with an electronic funds transfer.

_____16. A small business buys a new product line of inexpensive merchandise using a bank credit card.

_____17. A company gives a customer 60 days to pay for merchandise.

_____18. A company asks a new customer to make payment in advance.

_____19. A company has an arrangement with its bank to borrow cash for 30 days at 14% interest to cover its checking account whenever it is overdrawn due to expenses being greater than sales revenue.

_____20. An importer deposits cash in a bank so that a letter of credit can be given to an exporter.

Chapter 8 OUTLINE
Legal Agreements Around the World

GLOBAL FOCUS: TRADEMARKS, BRAND NAMES, AND INTERNATIONAL TRADE

LESSON 8-1 INTERNATIONAL LEGAL SYSTEMS AND LIABILITY

LEGAL SYSTEMS

CIVIL LAW

COMMON LAW

STATUTORY LAW

LIABILITY

LIABILITY FOR DEBT, LOSS, AND INJURY

PRODUCT LIABILITY

LESSON FEATURE
GLOBAL BUSINESS EXAMPLE: DIPLOMATIC IMMUNITY

LESSON 8-2 PROPERTY AND CONTRACTS

PROPERTY RIGHTS AND RESPONSIBILITIES

PROPERTY LAW

INTELLECTUAL PROPERTY

Patents

Trademarks

 ©South-Western Educational Publishing

Copyrights

CONTRACT LAW

COMPONENTS OF A CONTRACT

TREATIES AND TRADE AGREEMENTS

LESSON FEATURES
A QUESTION OF ETHICS: COUNTERFEIT PRODUCTS

COMMUNICATION ACROSS BORDERS: WHEN IS A CONTRACT NOT A CONTRACT?

LESSON 8-3 RESOLVING LEGAL DIFFERENCES

RESOLVING LEGAL DIFFERENCES WITHOUT COURT ACTION

MEDIATION

ARBITRATION

RESOLVING LEGAL DIFFERENCES USING COURT ACTION

LITIGATION

THE INTERNATIONAL COURT OF JUSTICE

LESSON FEATURES
GLOBAL BUSINESS EXAMPLE: LEGAL DIFFERENCES IN OTHER SOCIETIES

REGIONAL PERSPECTIVE: HISTORY: TAIWAN

 ©South-Western Educational Publishing

Lesson 8-1
International Legal Systems and Liability

LESSON QUIZ

Directions: For each of the following statements, if the statement is true, write a T on the answer line; if the statement is false, write an F on the answer line.

_____ 1. When a company does business in another country, it must observe its own country's laws, the host country's laws, and any treaties and trade agreements involving that country.

_____ 2. All countries enforce international law.

_____ 3. Statutes are usually passed in order to add to or change existing laws and to define laws for new situations that arise.

_____ 4. If you own a business, you are liable for the condition of the building.

_____ 5. The judicial systems in the United States and England are based on civil law.

_____ 6. Statutes are based on decisions made in previous legal cases.

_____ 7. Manufacturers are usually only liable for harm caused by their products if they intentionally caused the harm.

Directions: For each of the following items, decide which choice best completes the statement. Write the letter that identifies your choice on the answer line.

_____ 8. The type of legal system based on decisions made in prior cases is
   A. civil law.
   B. statutory law.
   C. common law.
   D. all of these

_____ 9. Common law is
   A. the basis of the legal system in the United States, England, and most of western Europe.
   B. based on commonly accepted principles that are then legislated as laws.
   C. a complete set of laws based on commonly accepted principles that are enacted as a single code.
   D. none of these

_____ 10. A liability for unpaid wages that are due to an employee for work performed is an example of
   A. product liability.
   B. strict liability.
   C. liability for debt, loss, and injury.
   D. all of these

_____ 11. Under strict liability laws, if a consumer uses gasoline to clean stains off clothing and then lights a match and suffers burns, the seller or manufacturer of the gasoline
   A. is liable under strict liability laws.
   B. is liable because there were no printed warnings not to light matches when using gasoline.
   C. is liable because the product was unreasonably dangerous to the user.
   D. none of these

Activity 1 • Identifying Liability

Directions: For each of the following situations, decide whether the situation involves a liability for debt loss or injury or for product liability under strict liability laws. Explain your answer.

1. A building entry is being renovated. Although there are tools, building supplies, and electrical cables scattered around the location, there are also large warning signs that the area is unsafe and under construction. Marge Thompson walks through the entry to satisfy her curiosity about the project, trips, and breaks a leg. Is either the building owner or contractor liable?

   _____

   _____

   _____

   _____

2. Ted Gordon is installing a built-in dishwasher. He studies the wiring instructions and determines how to connect the appliance to the home wiring system. He is interrupted by a long telephone conversation and when he returns to his installation he forgets that he did not turn off the current to the location and he also tries to connect the wrong wire to the positive house cable. He is shocked and suffers a broken leg when he falls from the shock. The dishwasher is also damaged. Is the manufacturer liable?

   _____

   _____

   _____

   _____

3. Melissa, a 6-year old, runs ahead of her parents at the zoo and climbs over a low guardrail and is bitten by a zoo animal. Is the zoo liable?

   _____

   _____

   _____

   _____

4. Mark Reinert is allergic to peanuts and products containing peanuts. His allergy is so sensitive that he may suffer shock if he eats peanuts. At a restaurant Mark orders a dinner and asks the server, who is a new employee of the restaurant, whether the dinner contains peanuts or is cooked with peanut oil. The server does not know how the dinner is prepared but knows it does not contain peanuts and tells Mark the dinner is safe. Mark spends the night in the emergency room. Is the restaurant liable?

   _____

   _____

   _____

   _____

5. Linda Aguilar cooks and serves to her family chicken from her refrigerator that she bought last week. The package label's expiration date is five days before Linda served it. Her family suffers food poisoning. Is the grocery store liable?

   _____

   _____

   _____

   _____

 ©South-Western Educational Publishing

Lesson 8-2
Property and Contracts

LESSON QUIZ

Directions: For each of the following statements, if the statement is true, write a T on the answer line; if the statement is false, write an F on the answer line.

_____ 1. Democratic countries generally recognize the individual's right to own property.

_____ 2. Non-democratic countries that wish to participate in international business usually recognize property rights in order to attract international business.

_____ 3. The World Intellectual Property Organization (WIPO) coordinates international treaties to protect patents, trademarks, and other intellectual property.

_____ 4. Patents protect the rights of inventors to profit from their inventions.

_____ 5. Trademarks can be protected in the home country, but there is no way to protect a trademark in other countries.

_____ 6. A trademark protects the inventor of a product or process for 17 years.

_____ 7. A contract is not enforceable if the terms of the contract call for breaking the law.

Directions: For each of the following items, decide which choice best completes the statement. Write the letter that identifies your choice on the answer line.

_____ 8. A person who makes duplicate copies of a videotape of a commercial movie and then sells it would be violating a
   A. patent.
   B. trademark.
   C. copyright.
   D. none of these

_____ 9. All of the following are essential components of a contract except
   A. mutual agreement.
   B. legal purpose.
   C. legal age.
   D. expressed in writing.

_____10. The term consideration used in regards to a contract means
   A. both parties agree to be considerate of each others' needs.
   B. something of value must be given by both parties.
   C. one party offers valid terms and the other party accepts them.
   D. none of these

_____11. International treaties and trade agreements may serve all the following purposes except
   A. allowing free flow of goods and services between member countries.
   B. helping to provide uniformity between different cultures and customs.
   C. setting currency exchange rates.
   D. helping to ensure fair competition practices between member countries.

Activity 1 • Identifying the Law That Applies

Directions: Read the examples in the left-hand column and write the area of law that protects that item in the right-hand column.

Item or Product	Area of Law That Protects the Item or Product
The invention of the CD player	
Coca-Cola®	
The script to the movie *The Wizard of Oz*	
A farm and machinery owned by a farmer	
The sale of a home by its owner	

Activity 2 • Analyzing Copyright Infringement

Directions: Colleen Dewitt has created a software program that solves a common business problem in a unique way. The program requires little computer memory and solves the problem with less effort than methods businesses are currently using. She has formed a company to market the software. Martin Bailey has made copies of the software and has repackaged it in a similar way and is selling it at a lower price as his own product. Analyze the effects of this copyright infringement on Colleen DeWitt, Martin Bailey, and society as a whole. Consider both positive and negative effects.

Colleen DeWitt, Creator	Society	Martin Bailey, Infringer

©South-Western Educational Publishing

Lesson 8-3
Resolving Legal Differences

LESSON QUIZ

Directions: For each of the following statements, if the statement is true, write a T on the answer line; if the statement is false, write an F on the answer line.

_____ 1. Throughout the world, most legal disputes have to be settled in court.

_____ 2. Business disputes are often settled in arbitration because a contract between the parties requires this method.

_____ 3. A mediator's decision does not need to be based on mutual agreement between the parties for it to be legal and binding.

_____ 4. Most countries have more than one court system, and the rules and procedures are usually different in each system.

_____ 5. When a government violates the terms of a contract with a foreign company, litigation usually occurs in the company's home country.

_____ 6. Arbitration and mediation are usually faster and less expensive than litigation.

_____ 7. To be in litigation is the same as being in arbitration.

Directions: For each of the following items, decide which choice best completes the statement. Write the letter that identifies your choice on the answer line.

_____ 8. The settlement of a dispute does not require the agreement of both parties in
A. mediation and arbitration.
B. arbitration and litigation.
C. mediation and litigation.
D. none of these

_____ 9. Of the following, the one that is not a reason for using mediation or arbitration instead of court action to settle a dispute is
A. to save time.
B. to follow legal procedures.
C. to avoid bad publicity.
D. to avoid the risk of discriminatory treatment in a foreign court.

_____ 10. A mediator does all of the following except
A. makes a binding decision.
B. makes suggestions and proposals.
C. helps the parties reach a compromise.
D. addresses the substance of the dispute.

_____ 11. In arbitration between parties in two different countries
A. the arbitrator may be an officer in a chamber of commerce or trade association for a third country.
B. the party who does not agree with the arbitrator's decision may pursue further litigation.
C. the host country party usually establishes the procedures for the arbitration.
D. none of these

Activity 1 • Comparing Methods of Dispute Resolution

Directions: For each of the three methods of dispute resolution, decide whether the method has the characteristic listed in the left column. Possible responses are Yes, No, Usually, and Not Usually.

	Characteristics	Mediation	Arbitration	Litigation
1.	Presider's decision is binding			
2.	Parties must agree to the decision			
3	Presider must be a judge			
4.	Relatively quick procedure			
5.	Decision must be based on the legal system			
6.	Expensive			

Activity 2 • Profiling a Career

Directions: Research one of the legal careers in the list below and write a summary of your findings on the form below. Use additional sheets of paper if needed. Choose from one of the following professions.

Arbitrator   **Judge**
Mediator   **Private investigator**
Attorney   **Legal secretary**
Paralegal

7. Job title _____

_____

8. Duties _____

_____

_____

_____

9. Education requirements _____

_____

_____

10. Future employment opportunities _____

_____

11. Salary expectations _____

_____

12. Skills needed _____

_____

_____

13. Opportunity for relocation in another country _____

_____

14. Differences in terminology or job requirements and duties that may exist in other countries _____

_____

Chapter 9 OUTLINE
Global Entrepreneurship and Small Business Management

GLOBAL FOCUS: A REAL CHIEF EXECUTIVE

LESSON 9-1 ENTREPRENEURIAL ENTERPRISES

THE ECONOMIC IMPORTANCE OF ENTREPRENEURS

INNOVATION AND THE ENTREPRENEURIAL SPIRIT

ECONOMIC AND SOCIAL BENEFITS OF SMALL BUSINESS

Small Businesses Are the Major Creators of New Products

Small Businesses Are the Major Source of New Jobs

Small Businesses Often Provide Personal Service

TYPES OF ENTREPRENEURIAL BUSINESSES

Agricultural, Mining, and Extracting Companies

Manufacturing Companies

Wholesalers

Retailers

Service Companies

FUTURE GROWTH FOR SMALL BUSINESS

HOME-BASED BUSINESSES

©South-Western Educational Publishing

Telecommuting

LESSON FEATURE
E-COMMERCE IN ACTION: INTERNET ENTREPRENEURS

LESSON 9-2 THE BUSINESS PLAN AND SELF-EMPLOYMENT

SELF-EMPLOYMENT AS A CAREER

ADVANTAGES OF SELF-EMPLOYMENT

DISADVANTAGES OF SELF-EMPLOYMENT

QUALITIES OF SUCCESSFUL ENTREPRENEURS

CREATING A BUSINESS PLAN

THE BUSINESS PLAN

Business Description

Organizational Structure

Marketing Activities

LESSON FEATURES
GLOBAL BUSINESS EXAMPLE: STREET ENTREPRENEURS IN LATIN AMERICA

REGIONAL PERSPECTIVE: GEOGRAPHY: AN UNCERTAIN FUTURE FOR THE WILDLIFE OF INDIA

©South-Western Educational Publishing

LESSON 9-3 OPERATING AN ENTREPRENEURIAL ENTERPRISE

FINANCING A SMALL BUSINESS

ANALYZING COSTS

BREAKEVEN POINT

SOURCES OF FUNDS

FINANCIAL RECORDS OF SMALL BUSINESSES

MANAGING THE SMALL BUSINESS

PRODUCTION MANAGEMENT

HUMAN RESOURCE MANAGEMENT

INFORMATION MANAGEMENT

LESSON FEATURES
GLOBAL BUSINESS EXAMPLE: FINANCING WOMEN ENTREPRENEURS IN NIGER

COMMUNICATION ACROSS BORDERS: CHOOSING A COMPANY LANGUAGE

 ©South-Western Educational Publishing

Lesson 9-1
Entrepreneurial Enterprises

LESSON QUIZ

Directions: For each of the following statements, if the statement is true, write a T on the answer line; if the statement is false, write an F on the answer line.

_____ 1. An entrepreneur is a person who owes money to a bank or other financial institution.

_____ 2. The major source of new jobs in the United States is large corporations that make products bought by millions of people.

_____ 3. Small businesses are too small to have any impact on the economy of a large country.

_____ 4. An extracting company changes raw materials and parts into usable products.

_____ 5. Consumers buy directly from retailers.

_____ 6. Experts predict that there are many areas in which there is room for great success by entrepreneurs in the coming years.

_____ 7. Telecommuting involves working in company offices using a computer, computer network, and other technology.

Directions: For each of the following items, decide which choice best completes the statement. Write the letter that identifies your choice on the answer line.

_____ 8. All of the following are economic or social benefits of entrepreneurial efforts except
   A. creating new products.
   B. providing personalized service.
   C. guaranteeing health insurance and retirement benefits.
   D. providing new jobs.

_____ 9. Wholesalers benefit the economy and other businesses by
   A. being intermediaries between producers and sellers.
   B. buying products from manufacturers.
   C. shipping products to retailers.
   D. all of these

_____10. All of the following are expected to be areas of growth for entrepreneurs except
   A. personal services.
   B. training workers to adapt to a changing workplace.
   C. health care services.
   D. automobile parts manufacturing.

_____11. All of the following statements describe advantages of telecommuting except
   A. with technology advances nearly every job can be done by telecommuting.
   B. telecommuting saves businesses money.
   C. government regulations may affect some kinds of home businesses.
   D. some valuable workers may remain with a company only if they can telecommute.

Activity 1 • Identifying Types of Entrepreneurial Businesses

Directions: For each of the following types of business enterprises, describe a company in your community (or create one).

1. Extracting company _____

_____

2. Manufacturing company _____

_____

3. Wholesaler _____

_____

4. Retailer _____

_____

5. Service company _____

_____

Activity 2 • Identifying Service Business Growth Opportunities

Directions: For each of the following types of services, use the *Yellow Pages* in your town, county, or nearest large city to identify three specialties in that kind of service. List the name and address of one company that offers one of the services.

6. Health care services: _____

_____

Name and address of one company: _____

_____

7. Environmental services: _____

_____

Name and address of one company: _____

_____

8. Training and education: _____

_____

Name and address of one company: _____

_____

9. Personal services: _____

_____

Name and address of one company: _____

_____

©South-Western Educational Publishing

Lesson 9-2
The Business Plan and Self-Employment

LESSON QUIZ

Directions: For each of the following statements, if the statement is true, write a T on the answer line; if the statement is false, write an F on the answer line.

_____ 1. Owning your own business has the advantage of career independence.

_____ 2. Burnout from working too hard for too many hours is a major reason why small-business owners sell their companies.

_____ 3. A good statement of a goal for a business would be to increase sales.

_____ 4. When a business's sales have peaked, the only way to make significant sales increases is to develop a new product idea.

_____ 5. Business knowledge is usually important for success as an entrepreneur.

_____ 6. A business plan is a guide that could be used to start and operate a company.

_____ 7. The only purpose of a business plan for a new business is to provide a guide or blueprint for the company's activities.

Directions: For each of the following items, decide which choice best completes the statement. Write the letter that identifies your choice on the answer line.

_____ 8. All of the following are advantages of owning a successful business except
   A. pride of ownership.
   B. independence.
   C. time commitment.
   D. gain in self-confidence.

_____ 9. All of the following are disadvantages of owning a business except
   A. setting goals.
   B. risk of losing investment.
   C. burnout.
   D. uncertain income.

_____ 10. All of the following are reasons for writing a business plan for a new business except
   A. to set goals or a plan of action for the business.
   B. to qualify for a bank loan.
   C. to persuade customers to buy the product.
   D. to attract new investors.

_____ 11. The organizational structure section of the business plan for a new business would include all of the following except
   A. whether the business is a sole proprietorship, partnership, or corporation.
   B. the price that will be charged for the company's product.
   C. any joint ventures or licensing agreements the company has.
   D. relationships with supplier.

Activity 1 • Rating Your Entrepreneurial Potential

Directions: For each of the following traits of successful entrepreneurs, rate yourself on the scales given.

1. **RISK TAKER**

| 1 | 2 | 3 | 4 | 5 |
Low   High

2. **SELF-CONFIDENT**

| 1 | 2 | 3 | 4 | 5 |
Low   High

3. **HARD WORKING**

| 1 | 2 | 3 | 4 | 5 |
Low   High

4. **GOAL-ORIENTED**

| 1 | 2 | 3 | 4 | 5 |
Low   High

5. **CREATIVE**

| 1 | 2 | 3 | 4 | 5 |
Low   High

6. **KNOWLEDGE OF BUSINESS**

| 1 | 2 | 3 | 4 | 5 |
Low   High

Activity 2 • Creating a Business Plan

Directions: For each category of a business plan listed below, provide a description for a company in your community or one you would like to start in the future.

7. Business description _____

_____

8. Organizational structure _____

_____

_____

9. Marketing activities _____

_____

_____

_____

_____

 ©South-Western Educational Publishing

Lesson 9-3
Operating an Entrepreneurial Enterprise

LESSON QUIZ

Directions: For each of the following statements, if the statement is true, write a T on the answer line; if the statement is false, write an F on the answer line.

_____ 1. A budget lists the current value of assets and liabilities of a business.

_____ 2. The salaries of office staff are an example of variable costs.

_____ 3. Raw materials are an example of a fixed cost for most companies.

_____ 4. Gross profit is calculated by subtracting the cost of an item from the selling price of the item.

_____ 5. The breakeven point is the number of items a company must sell so that there is neither a profit nor a loss.

_____ 6. Equity funds refer to money invested by the owners of a business.

_____ 7. A company with £50,000 of assets and £13,000 of liabilities would have a net worth of £37,000.

Directions: For each of the following items, decide which choice best completes the statement. Write the letter that identifies your choice on the answer line.

_____ 8. If the cost to produce an item is $15, its selling price is $20, and the total fixed costs are $100,000, the breakeven point is
   A. $5.
   B. 20,000 units.
   C. 5,000 units.
   D. impossible to calculate without additional information.

_____ 9. Cash sales, cash collected from customers on account, and cash obtained from loans or additional investments from owners are examples of
   A. assets.
   B. revenues.
   C. gross profit.
   D. cash inflows.

_____ 10. Human resource management involves
   A. hiring, training, and retaining employees.
   B. supervising employees.
   C. allocating resources so employees can do their jobs effectively.
   D. all of these

_____ 11. All of the following are part of a management information system plan except
   A. obtaining information.
   B. distributing reports to managers.
   C. planning cash flow.
   D. organizing information.

Activity 1 • Analyzing Business Financial Data

Directions: Drake Enterprises needs your assistance in preparing its financial statements. Sort the financial items and list them in the appropriate location on the balance sheet and income statement. *(You must complete this activity to be able to complete Activity 2.)*

Sales revenue	$350,000
Cash in bank	18,000
Selling expenses	163,000
Rent expense	60,000
Amount owed to suppliers	1,700
Salaries	88,000
Amount due from customers	4,500
Equipment	33,400
Amount owed for bank loan	3,000

Drake Enterprises
Balance Sheet
December 31, 20--

ASSETS	
LIABILITIES	
OWNER'S EQUITY (NET WORTH)	

Drake Enterprises
Income Statement
For the Year Ended December 31, 20--

REVENUE	
EXPENSES:	
NET INCOME	

©South-Western Educational Publishing

Chapter 9

Activity 2 • Analyzing Business Financial Statements

Directions: Answer the following questions about the financial statements of Drake Enterprises that you prepared in Activity 1.

1. What is the total amount of assets? _____

2. What is the net worth of the company? _____

3. How is net worth calculated? _____

4. What is the total of the expenses? _____

5. What is the amount of net income? _____

6. How is net income calculated? _____

    _____

7. What is it called if a company has more expenses than revenue? _____

    _____

8. How does net income affect a company's net worth? _____

    _____

9 How can you determine whether the amount of net income is a good result? _____

    _____

    _____

Activity 3 • Matching Types of Business Information

Directions: For each of the business information items listed below, place an A, B, C, or D to indicate whether the item is financial, production and inventory, marketing, or human resources information. Some items might relate to more than one type of information.

   A. financial information
   B. production and inventory information
   C. marketing information
   D. human resources information

_____10. health insurance records of employees

_____11. customer sales records

_____12. safety records of employee activities

_____13. parts needed for company products

_____14. raw materials list

_____15. operating budgets

_____16. information on competitor's products

_____17. job applications

_____18. government population reports

_____19. equipment repair records

Activity 4 • Creating a Business Plan

Directions: For each category of a business plan listed below, provide a description for a company in your community or one you would like to start in the future. You may continue the business you used in Activity 2 in Lesson 9-2 or choose a new business.

20. Financial planning _____

_____

_____

_____

_____

_____

_____

21. Production activities _____

_____

_____

_____

_____

_____

_____

22. Human resource activities _____

_____

_____

_____

_____

_____

_____

23. Information needs _____

_____

_____

_____

_____

_____

_____

 ©South-Western Educational Publishing

Chapter 10 OUTLINE
Management Principles in Action

GLOBAL FOCUS: VIRTUAL CORPORATIONS—HERE TODAY AND GONE TOMORROW

LESSON 10-1 MANAGERS AND CULTURAL DIFFERENCES

MANAGERS IN ORGANIZATIONS

CHARACTERISTICS OF MANAGERS

STYLES OF MANAGERS

Autocratic Management Style

Participative Management Style

Free-rein Management Style

INFLUENCES OF CULTURAL DIFFERENCES

Participation in Making Decisions

Hiring Preferences

Permanence of Employment

Labor-Management Relationships

LESSON FEATURES
A QUESTION OF ETHICS: SHARING CONFIDENTIAL INFORMATION

GLOBAL BUSINESS EXAMPLE: THE MANAGERS WHO REFUSED TO MAKE DECISIONS

LESSON 10-2 MANAGEMENT FUNCTIONS AND ORGANIZATION

PROCESS OF MANAGING

PLANNING AND DECISION MAKING

ORGANIZING, STAFFING, AND COMMUNICATING

MOTIVATING AND LEADING

CONTROLLING

STRUCTURES OF ORGANIZATIONS

ORGANIZATION BY FUNCTION

ORGANIZATION BY PRODUCT

ORGANIZATION BY GEOGRAPHY

LESSON FEATURE
E-COMMERCE IN ACTION: VIRTUAL BUSINESS PLANS

LESSON 10-3 THE CHANGING PROCESS OF MANAGEMENT

LEVELS OF MANAGEMENT

SPAN OF CONTROL

LINES OF AUTHORITY

DELEGATION OF AUTHORITY AND RESPONSIBILITY

EVOLUTION OF ORGANIZATIONS AND MANAGEMENT

STAGE ONE: DOMESTIC COMPANY

STAGE TWO: EXPORTING COMPANY

STAGE THREE: INTERNATIONAL CORPORATION

STAGE FOUR: GLOBAL CORPORATION

MANAGING NOW AND IN THE FUTURE

LESSON FEATURES
GLOBAL BUSINESS EXAMPLE: DOBRISKI ENTERPRISES

REGIONAL PERSPECTIVE: GEOGRAPHY: VATICAN CITY—HEADQUARTERS OF A WORLDWIDE CHURCH

©South-Western Educational Publishing

Lesson 10-1
Managers and Cultural Differences

LESSON QUIZ

Directions: For each of the following statements, if the statement is true, write a T on the answer line; if the statement is false, write an F on the answer line.

_____ 1. A virtual corporation comprises "the best of the best" units.

_____ 2. Autocratic, participative, and free-rein managers use power differently.

_____ 3. The autocratic style of management is usually the style employees work best under.

_____ 4. The participative management style is the one recommended for most situations today.

_____ 5. Every culture and subculture has norms for the behaviors of its members.

_____ 6. Workers in every culture regard permanence of employment very highly and prefer not to look for new opportunities.

_____ 7. Managers who consider the values, beliefs, and assumptions of the culture and subculture rather than those of individuals are generally the most successful in global business.

Directions: For each of the following items, decide which choice best completes the statement. Write the letter that identifies your choice on the answer line.

_____ 8. Leadership can be described as
   A. forcing people to do what you want them to do.
   B. gathering information to solve problems.
   C. the ability to get others to follow.
   D. the ability to use resources to achieve goals.

_____ 9. A manager who usually completes projects by ordering employees to do certain tasks but does not tell the employees how the tasks contribute to the project is
   A. an autocratic manager.
   B. a participative managers.
   C. a free-rein manager.
   D. a manager who combines several styles of management.

_____10. All of the following are actions that a participative manager would take except
   A. encourage employees to contribute ideas and suggestions.
   B. keep employees informed about project needs.
   C. give employees the opportunity to learn on their own and supply their own motivation.
   D. help employees set goals and ways to measure them.

_____11. All of the following statements describe behaviors that could be influenced by cultural differences except
   A. George Amarkos prefers to work in a local company where several of his relatives also work.
   B. Stacy Erickson buys all the products her company manufactures because she plans to work for the company until she retires in forty years.
   C. Mario Herrera is uncomfortable when his supervisor asks him for an opinion about a project at work.
   D. Oki Komuro does not like to work in an office that is air-conditioned.

Activity 1 • Identifying Types of Entrepreneurial Businesses

Directions: For Part A, determine the type of management style you would prefer in a supervisor. Then describe the effect of that style on the items that follow. In Part B, repeat the activity based on another style of management.

Part A: Preferred type of management style in a manager who supervises me

1. Management style _____

2. Meeting goals _____

_____

_____

3. Employee retention _____

_____

_____

4. Motivation _____

_____

_____

5. Creativity/originality _____

_____

_____

Part B: Another management style

6. Management style _____

7. Meeting goals _____

_____

_____

8. Employee retention _____

_____

_____

9. Motivation _____

_____

_____

10. Creativity/originality _____

_____

_____

©South-Western Educational Publishing

Lesson 10-2
Management Functions and Organization

LESSON QUIZ

Directions: For each of the following statements, if the statement is true, write a T on the answer line; if the statement is false, write an F on the answer line.

_____ 1. Planning is living with the consequences of decisions.

_____ 2. Leading is creating the desire to achieve, and motivating is getting employees to voluntarily pursue the goals of the organization.

_____ 3. Line positions are managerial, but staff positions are not.

_____ 4. Most organizations today are tall because so many managers are needed to accomplish complex goals.

_____ 5. Most businesses are not organized by function, product, or geography.

_____ 6. A company with several different departments should always organize by function.

_____ 7. A global business would most often organize by geography and then by product.

Directions: For each of the following items, decide which choice best completes the statement. Write the letter that identifies your choice on the answer line.

_____ 8. All of the following are examples of the controlling function of management except
   A. taking preventive and corrective actions.
   B. motivating employees.
   C. using outside auditors to review accounting records.
   D. adjusting inputs to maximize outputs.

_____ 9. An organization with many levels of management is described as
   A. tall.
   B. flat.
   C. organized by geography.
   D. none of these

_____10. Staff positions are those that
   A. supervise people and resources.
   B. assist managers in line positions.
   C. are near the top of the organizational chart.
   D. none of these

_____11. A company that is organized into separate divisions for paper products, plastic products, and metal products is an example of
   A. organization by function.
   B. organization by product.
   C. organization by geography.
   D. organization by division.

Activity 1 • Creating an Organizational Chart

Directions: Draw an organizational chart for Futures Unlimited based upon the following information.

Amir Amin is president and chief executive officer of Futures Unlimited. Futures Unlimited has two divisions.

The Talent Division is managed by Lori Wong. She supervises the three departments that constitute the Talent Division. The departments are the Eastern Department which has five employees; the Central Department which has two employees, and the Western Department which has three employees.

The Production Division is managed by Stephen Wolfe. He supervises the Photographic and the Print departments, each of which has three employees.

Lesson 10-3
The Changing Process of Management

LESSON QUIZ

Directions: For each of the following statements, if the statement is true, write a T on the answer line; if the statement is false, write an F on the answer line.

_____ 1. The number of managers a business needs depends on the size of the business and the complexity of its operations.

_____ 2. An organizational chart shows only the managers within the organization.

_____ 3. The delegation of authority and responsibility is transferring authority and responsibility to others.

_____ 4. When authority and responsibility are widely distributed among many employees and organizational units, the management is considered to be centralized.

_____ 5. A domestic company must know a lot of information about a foreign market to expand into being an exporting company.

_____ 6. In an international corporation a parent company provides an organizational structure of local, national, or regional subsidiaries that are usually responsible for decision making and customer service.

_____ 7. Managing a global business tomorrow is expected to be different from managing a typical business today.

Directions: For each of the following items, decide which choice best completes the statement. Write the letter that identifies your choice on the answer line.

_____ 8. A manager who oversees the day-to-day operations in a specific department is a
   A. front-line manager.
   B. middle manager.
   C. senior manager.
   D. all of these

_____ 9. Lines of authority
   A. are usually less clearly understood in a small sole proprietorship.
   B. indicate who is responsible to whom and for what.
   C. are not as important in a larger business where people work as teams.
   D. none of these

_____ 10. All of the following are characteristics needed by managers of the future global corporation except
   A. able to manage transition and change in a culturally diverse world.
   B. able to quickly adapt to a changing environment.
   C. able to function as part of a team.
   D. able to make quick decisions without regard to consequences for other managers.

Activity 1 • Identifying Characteristics of Businesses

Directions: For each of the following phrases, place a check mark in the one column that is the best description of the kind of company or corporation indicated by the phrase.

		Domestic Company	Export Company	International Corporation	Global Corporation
1.	Manufactures and sells in the same country				
2.	Sometimes called a multinational corporation				
3.	Relies on domestic competitive advantages while selling abroad				
4.	Buys and sells with little or no regard for national boundaries				
5.	Often uses independent agents or distributors				
6.	Transacts business with local residents only				
7.	Is an outgrowth of an international (or multinational) corporation				
8.	Creates and markets goods and services in several countries				

Activity 2 • Analyzing a Career as a Manager

Directions: Answer the following questions regarding your future career as a manager.

9. Not everyone is suited to being a manager. However, assume that your career goal is to be a manager. Would you rather be a front-line, middle, or senior manager? Explain your choice. _____

_____

_____

10. What are three industries you might like to work as a manager in? _____

_____

11. What education level and which specific courses do you think would best prepare you for the managerial job you've described? _____

_____

_____

12. What management style is best suited to your personality? Why? _____

_____

_____

_____

 ©South-Western Educational Publishing

Chapter 11 OUTLINE
Human Resources Management

GLOBAL FOCUS: I WANT TO GO HOME

LESSON 11-1 FOUNDATIONS OF HUMAN RESOURCES MANAGEMENT

GLOBAL HUMAN RESOURCE MANAGEMENT

WHO MAKES UP THE LABOR MARKET?

FOUR HUMAN RESOURCES MANAGEMENT APPROACHES

ETHNOCENTRIC APPROACH

POLYCENTRIC APPROACH

REGIOCENTRIC APPROACH

GEOCENTRIC APPROACH

LESSON 11-2 SELECTING AND TRAINING STAFF

DETERMINING STAFFING NEEDS

RECRUITING POTENTIAL EMPLOYEES

SELECTING QUALIFIED EMPLOYEES

Competence

Adaptability

Personal Characteristics

●

LESSON FEATURES
GLOBAL BUSINESS EXAMPLE: IBM USES MODERN-DAY HEADHUNTERS

REGIONAL PERSPECTIVE: HISTORY: THE MERCHANT-VENTURERS OF BRISTOL

LESSON 11-3 MAXIMIZATION OF HUMAN RESOURCES

TRAINING AND DEVELOPMENT ARE CRITICAL

●

MAJOR EXPENSE

TYPES OF TRAINING AND DEVELOPMENT

JOB-RELATED ISSUES

●

Language and Relationship Issues

Cross-Cultural Training

Spousal Employment Counseling

TRAINING AND DEVELOPMENT HELP TO PREVENT FAILURE

WHY GLOBAL EMPLOYEES FAIL

REDUCING THE CHANCE OF EMPLOYEE FAILURE

LESSON FEATURES
GLOBAL BUSINESS EXAMPLE: AUSTRALIAN EMPLOYERS MUST TRAIN EMPLOYEES

GLOBAL BUSINESS EXAMPLE: LANGUAGE MATTERS IN FRANCE

LESSON 11-4 RETAINING HUMAN RESOURCES

CULTURAL EMPLOYEE MOTIVATION

COMPENSATING EMPLOYEES

Cultural Sensitivity

Base Salary

Expatriate Bonus

Cost-of-Living Adjustment

Employee Benefits

EVALUATING EMPLOYEE PERFORMANCE

ANTICIPATING REPATRIATION

LESSON FEATURE
A QUESTION OF ETHICS: THE COMPANY PICNIC THAT BOMBED

©South-Western Educational Publishing

Lesson 11-1
Foundations of Human Resource Management

LESSON QUIZ

Directions: For each of the following statements, if the statement is true, write a T on the answer line; if the statement is false, write an F on the answer line.

_____ 1. Sam Hogan was born and raised in England. When he works in the United States he is an expatriate.

_____ 2. Maria Gonzales was born and raised in Mexico and works in a Canadian company's New York City office. Maria is considered a parent-country national.

_____ 3. When staffing a new office in a different country, it is always better to hire local natives of that country because they are usually culturally sensitive and easy to find.

_____ 4. There are four major approaches to human resource management in the global environment.

_____ 5. The approach to human resource management used by a company has little bearing on the nationalities of company employees.

_____ 6. Sometimes a less-developed country will benefit from a foreign company that uses the ethnocentric approach.

_____ 7. A disadvantage of the polycentric approach to human resource management is the cultural gap between the headquarters and subsidiary managers.

Directions: For each of the following items, decide which choice best completes the statement. Write the letter that identifies your choice on the answer line.

_____ 8. All of the following statements describe factors involved in hiring parent-country nationals to staff a foreign subsidiary except
   A. they may have the desired company orientation, knowledge, and skills.
   B. they may be more costly than other types of employees.
   C. they will probably be acceptable to locals.
   D. local laws may restrict hiring these employees.

_____ 9. The type of human resources approach that uses natives of the host country to manage operations within their country and parent-country natives to manage at headquarters is the
   A. ethnocentric approach.
   B. polycentric approach.
   C. regiocentric approach.
   D. geocentric approach.

_____ 10. The type of human resources approach that uses the best available managers without regard for their countries of origin is the
   A. ethnocentric approach.
   B. polycentric approach.
   C. regiocentric approach.
   D. geocentric approach.

Activity 1 • Defining Human Resource Practices Around the World
Directions: Complete the following table by supplying the missing information related to the nationalities and human resource approach for the multinational companies listed.

HUMAN RESOURCE PRACTICES AROUND THE WORLD

	Company	Home Country	Nationalities of Managers		Human Resource Approach
			Headquarters	Subsidiaries	
1.	A-OK, Inc.	United States		All	Geocentric
2.	Backe	Germany	German	German French British Dutch Swedish Danish	
3.	Tewks, Ltd.	United Kingdom		Belgian British Canadian Australian	Polycentric
4.	Étoile	France	French		Ethnocentric
5.	Nippon	Japan	Japanese	Japanese	
6.	Mantequilla, S.A.	Mexico	Mexican American Canadian	Mexican American Canadian	

©South-Western Educational Publishing
Chapter 11

Lesson 11-2
Selecting and Training Staff

LESSON QUIZ

Directions: For each of the following statements, if the statement is true, write a T on the answer line; if the statement is false, write an F on the answer line.

_____ 1. Employers use employment forecasting and supply analysis to determine their staffing needs.

_____ 2. Staffing the varied positions at home and abroad with culturally sensitive and technically competent employees is demanding work.

_____ 3. Both the human resource management approach and the type of work to be performed influence the choice of recruiting outlets.

_____ 4. The best applicant for a job as an engineer is the person with the highest level of technical knowledge and skill.

_____ 5. The characteristics of a job applicant's family may be an important consideration for a position in a foreign country.

_____ 6. Most applicants are screened based on their competence, adaptability, and personality characteristics.

_____ 7. When hiring for an international position, a company always hires the applicant who has the best combination of competence, adaptability, and personal characteristics even if the applicant is weak in some areas.

Directions: For each of the following items, decide which choice best completes the statement. Write the letter that identifies your choice on the answer line.

_____ 8. A job description should include all of the following information except
A. the identification or title of the job.
B. the education and experience requirements of the job.
C. the marital status and family characteristics required for the job.
D. the duties and responsibilities of the job.

_____ 9. All of the following are dimensions of the factor of competence for a position in another country except
A. cultural awareness and language skills.
B. technical knowledge and experience.
C. desire to work abroad.
D. leadership and the ability to manage.

_____ 10. All of the following are dimensions of the factor of personal characteristics for a position in another country except
A. maturity.
B. social acceptability.
C. tactfulness.
D. foreign language fluency.

Activity 1 • Screening Prospective Employees

Directions: During the screening process the qualifications of job applicants are carefully investigated. Place a check mark in the appropriate column to indicate whether each of the following screening activities provides information primarily about the applicant's competence, adaptability, or personal characteristics.

	Screening Activity	Competence	Adaptability	Personal Characteristics
1.	Requesting a written statement from a former supervisor about the applicant's technical knowledge			
2.	Asking an applicant if he or she has ever lived abroad			
3.	Asking an applicant if he or she speaks the language of the country where the job is located			
4.	Asking an applicant about her or his physical health as it relates to job requirements			
5.	Asking a former employer of the applicant to verify the number of years that the applicant worked for the company			
6.	Asking the applicant if he or she has ever worked closely with members of a specified ethnic group			
7.	Asking an applicant about the family's willingness to live abroad			
8.	Asking an applicant about her or his personal strengths and weaknesses			
9.	Asking an applicant to justify the use of an alternate managerial style			
10.	Asking the applicant about the business climate in the foreign country where the job is located			

©South-Western Educational Publishing

Lesson 11-3
Maximization of Human Resources

LESSON QUIZ

Directions: For each of the following statements, if the statement is true, write a T on the answer line; if the statement is false, write an F on the answer line.

_____ 1. Training and development have little influence on the success of a company in the global marketplace.

_____ 2. Companies that provide training and development for employees on international assignments are usually more successful than those that do not.

_____ 3. Cross-cultural training includes providing information about local currency, foods, housing, and living costs.

_____ 4. Failure to provide appropriate training to a parent-country national may cause the employee to be angry and frustrated and want to return home sooner than expected.

_____ 5. A company that provides parent-country nationals and their families with training and development is wasting its money.

_____ 6. Family-related problems rarely cause parent-country nationals to fail in international assignments.

_____ 7. A good strategy for an employee who is dissatisfied and not very successful is to assign him or her to an overseas assignment for a new challenge.

Directions: For each of the following items, decide which choice best completes the statement. Write the letter that identifies your choice on the answer line.

_____ 8. Training and development programs
   A. are usually provided for all employees.
   B. are a strength of U.S.-based international companies today and in the past.
   C. are so expensive that a company usually carefully selects the employees for these programs.
   D. all of these

_____ 9. Job-related issues training for international employees addresses all of the following except
   A. relevant government policies and regulations.
   B. employment opportunities for a spouse.
   C. current economic and legal environments.
   D. information about subsidiaries and their operations.

_____ 10. The chances of employee failure on an overseas assignment can be reduced by all of the following practices except
   A. providing training before, during, and after the assignment.
   B. making international assignments part of the long-term employee development process.
   C. providing a job that use the employee's international experience when the employee returns from the assignment.
   D. providing extra compensation for taking an international assignment.

Activity 1 • Analyzing Daily Life in Another Country

Directions: Locate information related to daily life in another country that is very different from your country. Use a recent newspaper, magazine article, web site, or television or radio news report. If the source is a printed article, attach a copy to this page if possible. Then answer the following questions. (Hint: Travel magazines and *National Geographic* may be good sources of articles.)

1. Source of information _____

   _____

2. Date of article or report _____

3. How would you rate the reliability of your source? Why? _____

   _____

4. Describe the food in this country and how people shop for it. _____

   _____

   _____

   _____

   _____

5. How would you adapt to the food situation if you were assigned to this country? _____

   _____

   _____

   _____

6. Describe the housing conditions and availability in this country. _____

   _____

   _____

   _____

   _____

7. How would you adapt to the housing situation if you were assigned to this country? _____

   _____

   _____

8. Describe the recreation and entertainment opportunities in this country. _____

   _____

   _____

   _____

   _____

9. How would you adapt to the recreation and entertainment situation if you were assigned to this country?

   _____

   _____

   _____

©South-Western Educational Publishing

Lesson 11-4
Retaining Human Resources

LESSON QUIZ

Directions: For each of the following statements, if the statement is true, write a T on the answer line; if the statement is false, write an F on the answer line.

_____ 1. U.S. workers value taking personal risks to gain personal rewards; therefore, financial rewards are always the strongest motivating tool for all U.S. employees.

_____ 2. It is possible in some cultures to offend an employee by giving public praise for outstanding achievement.

_____ 3. When an international company designs a compensation package it should apply equally to all employees in all company offices.

_____ 4. A cost-of-living adjustment is a way to adjust an employee's compensation up or down to reflect the relative cost of living in a different location.

_____ 5. When an employee's performance is being evaluated, one factor to consider is the difficulty of the tasks assigned.

_____ 6. Expatriates should begin planning for their return before they even travel abroad.

_____ 7. What motivates employees in one country will usually motivate employees in every other country in which a company does business.

Directions: For each of the following items, decide which choice best completes the statement. Write the letter that identifies your choice on the answer line.

_____ 8. All of the following statements about money as a motivating factor are true except
   A. money is seen by U.S. employees as a reward for taking risks.
   B. money is a major motivating factor for most U.S. employees.
   C. in addition to money, other factors such as personal recognition, are also motivating factors for many U.S. workers.
   D. the U.S. model of money as a motivating factor is dominant throughout the world.

_____ 9. Evaluating employee performance in company offices around the world
   A. should be tailored to meet local environment, task, and individual personality differences.
   B. may present a challenge in cultures in which evaluation is seen as a lack of trust.
   C. may use different standards and forms in different countries even in the same company.
   D. all of these

_____ 10. Additions to employee compensation may include
   A. transportation.
   B. vacation trips.
   C. anything that is legal.
   D. all of these

_____ 11. All of the following are ways of minimizing problems in repatriation except
   A. being grateful for experiences abroad as a way of appreciating the home culture.
   B. keeping foreign experiences private because old friends will not understand them.
   C. planning in advance for employment after returning home.
   D. exploring job options with other companies.

.

Activity 1 • Designing a Compensation Plan

Directions: For each of the following situations, list items that could be included in a compensation plan to persuade the employee to accept a position in the new country and to motivate the employee to do an outstanding job. You may be creative and use ideas that were not listed in the textbook.

1. Mark Singer is an expert in telecommunications and is needed for a long-term assignment of several years in Tokyo. He and his wife are avid golfers when they are not both immersed in their careers. They have a daughter in college in a different state and are active in community arts groups. They have dinner every Friday night at the restaurant where they had their first date.

_____

_____

_____

_____

2. Melissa Tanaki is the top statistical analyst in the corporation. She is fluent in Spanish and needed for a long-term assignment in Brazil. Her interests include gourmet cooking, collecting pottery, and tennis. She has been thinking of purchasing a luxury condominium.

_____

_____

_____

_____

Activity 2 • Analyzing Your Compensation Needs

Directions: Assume that you are a recent college graduate with an excellent record and skills that are in high demand. You are being interviewed and pursued by several companies who are competing for you by offering enhancements to a compensation package. List five fringe benefits that a company could provide for you that would match your personal interests or desires and persuade you to accept that company's offer over another company's offer, all other factors being equal. Then complete the table to indicate an estimated cost of providing that benefit and the likelihood that a company would be willing to provide it.

Desired Fringe Benefits	Estimated Cost To Provide	Likelihood of Providing		
		Low	Medium	High

Chapter 12 OUTLINE
International Career Planning

GLOBAL FOCUS: A GLOBAL BUSINESS CAREER

LESSON 12-1 SEARCHING FOR YOUR FIRST JOB

CAREER PLANNING

THE IMPORTANCE OF WORK

FIVE STEPS IN CAREER PLANNING

Step 1 Determine Your Personal Goals and Abilities

Step 2 Evaluate the Job Market

Step 3 Identify and Apply for Specific Job Opportunities

Step 4 Accept the Most Desirable Job Offer

Step 5 Plan for Personal Career Development

EXPLORING CAREER INFORMATION

Library Materials

Media

Personal and Business Contacts

Community Organizations

Internet

IDENTIFYING CAREER OPPORTUNITIES

FACTORS AFFECTING CAREER CHOICE

Personal Factors

Demographic Trends

Geographic Influences

 ©South-Western Educational Publishing

Economic Conditions

Industry Trends

SOURCES OF AVAILABLE JOBS

LESSON FEATURE
E-COMMERCE IN ACTION: WIDEYES

LESSON 12-2 APPLYING FOR A JOB

CREATING A RESUME

Personal Data

Career Objective

Experience

Related Activities

Education

Honors and Awards

References

OTHER JOB APPLICATION DOCUMENTS

DEVELOPING A COVER LETTER

COMPLETING AN APPLICATION FORM

SECURING INTERNATIONAL EMPLOYMENT DOCUMENTS

INTERVIEWING FOR A JOB

BEFORE YOU INTERVIEW

WHEN YOU INTERVIEW

 ©South-Western Educational Publishing

AFTER YOU INTERVIEW

LESSON FEATURES
GLOBAL BUSINESS EXAMPLE: CROSS-CULTURAL INTERVIEWING

COMMUNICATION ACROSS BORDERS: DRESSING UP FOR THE BRITISH

LESSON 12-3 OBTAINING FUTURE JOBS

DEVELOPING CAREER OPTIONS

TRAINING OPPORTUNITIES

CAREER ADVANCEMENT

CHANGING CAREERS

PREPARING FOR INTERNATIONAL CAREERS

UNDERSTAND YOURSELF

STRENGTHEN YOUR FOUNDATIONAL SKILLS

ENHANCE YOUR LANGUAGE SKILLS

DEVELOP RELEVANT KNOWLEDGE, SKILLS, AND ATTITUDES

General Education

Business Education

GAIN INTERNATIONAL EXPERIENCE

NETWORK WITH INTERNATIONAL PROFESSIONALS

LESSON FEATURES
GLOBAL BUSINESS EXAMPLE: WHAT IS AN EXPORT-RELATED JOB?

REGIONAL PERSPECTIVE: HISTORY: THE BUBONIC PLAGUE

 ©South-Western Educational Publishing

Lesson 12-1
Searching for Your First Job

LESSON QUIZ

Directions: For each of the following statements, if the statement is true, write a T on the answer line; if the statement is false, write an F on the answer line.

_____1. A job is a commitment to a profession that requires continued training and has a clear path for advancement.

_____ 2. The only reason for working is to earn money to pay for the physical necessities of living and for desired luxuries.

_____ 3. When faced with several job offers, the best offer to accept may not be the one that pays the most.

_____ 4. Talking with people can be a valuable way to learn about careers.

_____ 5. The location of natural resources usually has little effect on where jobs are available.

_____ 6. Technology has decreased the need for workers who understand and can use computers.

_____ 7. Visiting companies can be a source of available jobs that may not be advertised to the general public.

Directions: For each of the following items, decide which choice best completes the statement. Write the letter that identifies your choice on the answer line.

_____ 8. All of the following are steps in the career planning process except
   A. obtaining additional education and training after you begin a career to prepare for possible career or company changes.
   B. determining what kinds of jobs are available.
   C. creating an Internet web site to promote a personal interest.
   D. assessing your abilities.

_____ 9. Using the Internet to search for a job
   A. never costs anything.
   B. includes posting your resume for employers to review.
   C. only applies to technical or computer-related jobs.
   D. all of these

_____10. Career choice and the availability of different kinds of jobs are affected by several factors including
   A. demographics, such as an increase in average life span.
   B. economic conditions, such as changing consumer demands.
   C. personal factors, such as the education and experience required for a specific job.
   D. all of these

Activity 1 • Identifying International Business Career Opportunities

Directions: For the following global business situations, list new international business jobs that might be created.

1. A computer manufacturer in France enters into a joint venture with a software company in Mexico.

_____

_____

_____

2. A nation passes a new law that requires that 60 percent of the parts in any products made in the country must be from within the country.

_____

_____

_____

3. A nation agrees to lower its tariffs on imported products.

_____

_____

_____

4. A nation has a very high inflation rate.

_____

_____

_____

Activity 2 • Using Career Planning Information Sources

Directions: For each of the five sources of career planning information listed, describe how you might use it in the future to research a job opportunity.

5. Library materials _____

_____

_____

6. Personal and business contacts _____

_____

_____

7. Media _____

_____

_____

8. Community organizations _____

_____

_____

9. Internet _____

_____

_____

Lesson 12-2
Applying for a Job

LESSON QUIZ

Directions: For each of the following statements, if the statement is true, write a T on the answer line; if the statement is false, write an F on the answer line.

_____ 1. The job application process involves communicating with a prospective employer via a resume, application letter, and interview.

_____ 2. A resume should list all of the classes you have taken.

_____ 3. The main purpose of an application letter is to obtain background information about a company.

_____ 4. A passport allows a person to work in another country.

_____ 5. Business attire, such as a suit, is almost always the most appropriate attire to wear to a job interview.

_____ 6. A screening interview usually involves general questions to determine if a person is suitable for employment.

_____ 7. Interviewers do not usually want job applicants to ask questions during an interview.

_____ 8. The purpose of a follow-up letter after an interview is to resell yourself and stand out in a positive way from others who were interviewed.

Directions: For each of the following items, decide which choice best completes the statement. Write the letter that identifies your choice on the answer line.

_____ 9. The experience section of a resume should include all of the following except
    A. a description of the major job duties of past jobs held.
    B. the salary earned in past jobs held.
    C. employers' names and addresses for current and past jobs.
    D. community service activities that were similar to a job.

_____ 10. A resume should include all of the following information except
    A. past job duties described using action verbs.
    B. awards and honors.
    C. specific courses that are relevant to the job.
    D. marital background.

_____ 11. It is useful to bring a personal data sheet to an employment interview because
    A. the information can be used to fill out a job application form accurately.
    B. you might not have prepared a resume.
    C. the employer may ask for one.
    D. none of these

_____ 12. The chances of having a successful employment interview are increased if you
    A. do practice interviews to improve your skills.
    B. arrive early and try to relax.
    C. research the company and prepare questions to ask the interviewer.
    D. all of these

Activity 1 • Answering Common Interview Questions

Directions: Seven questions that often are asked during an interview are listed below. Prepare answers to the questions to help you prepare for future job interviews.

1. What experience and training have prepared you for this job? _____
_____
_____
_____

2. Besides going to school, how have you expanded your knowledge and interests? _____
_____
_____
_____
_____

3. What did you like best about school? What did you like least? _____
_____
_____
_____
_____

4. In what types of situations do you get frustrated? _____
_____
_____
_____
_____

5. What are your major strengths? major weaknesses? What have you done to overcome your weaknesses?
_____
_____
_____
_____

6. What do you believe makes a successful person? _____
_____
_____
_____
_____

7. Describe the work situation you would like to have five years from now. _____
_____
_____
_____

Lesson 12-3
Obtaining Future Jobs

LESSON QUIZ

Directions: For each of the following statements, if the statement is true, write a T on the answer line; if the statement is false, write an F on the answer line.

_____ 1. Although it is useful to learn new skills to advance a career, changing technology may require learning new skills.

_____ 2. As careers develop, people seek new challenges, increased responsibility, and greater rewards.

_____ 3. Most people only have one or two different jobs in their entire lives.

_____ 4. Technology or company changes may eliminate a job and require a person to find a new position.

_____ 5. It is usually only necessary to have a strong grasp of English language skills to be successful in an international career because English is the language of international business.

_____ 6. General education courses such as geography, history, and mathematics are important to success in a career in international business.

_____ 7. The only way to gain international experiences is to travel or live in another country.

Directions: For each of the following items, decide which choice best completes the statement. Write the letter that identifies your choice on the answer line.

_____ 8. People can prepare for international careers by
   A. strengthening their foundational skills.
   B. traveling in foreign countries.
   C. improving leadership and administration skills.
   D. all of these

_____ 9. Networking with international professionals can be achieved by
   A. joining a professional organization that has members with international experience.
   B. talking with expatriates who have recently returned from international assignments.
   C. interacting with people from other countries who live and work in the immediate area.
   D. all of these

_____ 10. People can obtain relevant international experiences
   A. only through travel to foreign countries.
   B. only by reading about other cultures and studying languages if international travel is not possible.
   C. by participating in local groups that serve diverse ethnic groups.
   D. none of these

Activity 1 • Analyzing Community Resources for Development

Directions: For each of the following areas, describe resources in your community for developing knowledge or skills in that area. Use local newspapers, libraries, telephone directories, the Internet, and personal knowledge to complete this activity.

1. Foreign language skills _____
   _____
   _____

2. Communication skills _____
   _____
   _____

3. Technical skills _____
   _____
   _____

4. Marketing skills _____
   _____
   _____

Activity 2 • Analyzing Networking with International Professionals

Directions: Use your knowledge of your community, any available reference materials or other publications, and the personal knowledge of you and your friends to describe ways you could network with international professionals. Do not overlook relatives, family friends, and local businesses. Include a strategy for using or approaching one of these resources yourself.

5. Resources for networking
   _____
   _____
   _____
   _____
   _____
   _____
   _____

6. Personal strategy for using one of these resources
   _____
   _____
   _____
   _____
   _____
   _____

 ©South-Western Educational Publishing

Chapter 13 OUTLINE
Organized Labor

GLOBAL FOCUS: SOLIDARITY IN POLAND

LESSON 13-1 MILESTONES OF THE LABOR MOVEMENT

FORMATION OF LABOR UNIONS

LABOR UNIONS IN THE UNITED STATES

LEGAL STATUS OF THE FIRST UNIONS

LEGAL STATUS OF UNIONS TODAY

LABOR UNIONS IN OTHER COUNTRIES

UNIONS PAST AND PRESENT

EVOLUTION OF THE AFL-CIO

MEMBERSHIP IN UNIONS TODAY

LESSON FEATURES
GLOBAL BUSINESS EXAMPLE: THE NOBLE ORDER OF THE KNIGHTS OF LABOR

REGIONAL PERSPECTIVE: HISTORY: UNIONS IN THE UNITED KINGDOM

©South-Western Educational Publishing

LESSON 13-2 UNIONS IN THE WORKPLACE TODAY

ACHIEVING UNION REPRESENTATION

ELECTIONS

TYPES OF UNION REPRESENTATION

TOOLS OF LABOR NEGOTIATIONS

GRIEVANCE PROCEDURE

ARBITRATION

STRIKES

MANAGEMENT AND LABOR UNIONS

WHEN UNIONS AND MANAGEMENT WORK TOGETHER

LESSON FEATURES
GLOBAL BUSINESS EXAMPLE: THE SAD BUT REAL THING

A QUESTION OF ETHICS: INTERNATIONAL STRIKEBREAKERS

E-COMMERCE IN ACTION: PINNACLE PLC GOES ELECTRONIC

 ©South-Western Educational Publishing

Lesson 13-1
Milestones of the Labor Movement

LESSON QUIZ
Directions: For each of the following statements, if the statement is true, write a T on the answer line; if the statement is false, write an F on the answer line.

_____ 1. Injunctions have been used by employers to prevent or discourage union activity.

_____ 2. Firefighters and police officers almost always have the right to strike included in their contracts because it is the only way they can have any bargaining power with an employer the size of government.

_____ 3. Originally, unions were organized along industrial lines.

_____ 4. While union membership has declined in the United States, it has increased in all other developed countries.

_____ 5. In Germany, unions are organized along industry lines.

_____ 6. A union of bricklayers is an example of a craft union.

_____ 7. Nearly half of all U.S. workers belong to a union.

Directions: For each of the following items, decide which choice best completes the statement. Write the letter that identifies your choice on the answer line.

_____ 8. The labor policy of codetermination means that
   A. companies determine labor policies.
   B. union members serve on the boards of directors of corporations.
   C. union officers are determined by a company election.
   D. none of these

_____ 9. In the United States the AFL-CIO
   A. uses its size and resources to affect legislation that affects its members.
   B. is an organization of many unions.
   C. consists of most unions in the United States today.
   D. all of these

_____10. All of the following are reasons why union membership has declined in most countries except for which statement.
   A. Manufacturing industries are such a large part of a country's economy.
   B. Service businesses have become a larger part of most economies and unions have little experience in organizing service industry workers.
   C. Working conditions in service businesses are very different from those in manufacturing businesses.
   D. Governments have enacted legislation that protects workers.

Activity 1 • Analyzing Labor Relations Data

Directions: Analyze the data in the table. Use the information to answer the questions that follow.

UNION MEMBERSHIP IN THE UNITED STATES IN 1999
CATEGORIZED BY SELECTED CHARACTERISTICS

Category	Total Work force	Union Members	Percentage of Total Workforce That Belongs to a Union
16-24 year olds	19,606,000	1,110,000	
25-34 year olds	28,657,000	3,415,000	
35-44 year olds	32,438,000	4,918,000	
45-54 year olds	24,665,000	4,881,000	
55-64 year olds	10,880,000	1,932,000	
Women	57,050,000	6,528,000	
Men	61,914,000	9,949,000	
African American	14,346,000	2,463,000	
Hispanic	12,810,000	1,525,000	
Caucasian	99,147,000	13,349,000	

Source: Bureau of Labor Statistics, 2000. http://stats.bls.gov/news.release/union2.t-1.htm.

1. Complete the last column of the table above. Round calculations to the nearest tenth of a percent.

2. Which racial/ethnic group has the highest percentage of membership in unions?

   _____

3. Do more women or men belong to unions? Proportionately, which gender has greater union membership?

   _____

   _____

4. What was the total number of workers represented by unions in 1999?

   _____

   _____

5. What percentage of the total work force belonged to a union in 1999?

   _____

   _____

6. Are younger people or older people more likely to be union members?

   _____

   _____

   _____

Lesson 13-2
Unions in the Workplace Today

LESSON QUIZ

Directions: For each of the following statements, if the statement is true, write a T on the answer line; if the statement is false, write an F on the answer line.

_____ 1. Today, closed shops are generally illegal.

_____ 2. From the union's point of view, the most attractive arrangement is the open shop.

_____ 3. The topics of collective bargaining negotiations are legally restricted to wages and hours of work.

_____ 4. A lockout occurs when workers refuse to work.

_____ 5. In general, unions reduce a manager's freedom to act and make decisions.

_____ 6. If a union has a large strike fund, it can support workers on strike for a longer period.

_____ 7. Over the years, the number of strikes, the number of workers involved in strikes, and the number of days lost due to strikes in the United States have increased.

_____ 8. As the production process becomes more automated, the effectiveness of strikes declines.

Directions: For each of the following items, decide which choice best completes the statement. Write the letter that identifies your choice on the answer line.

_____ 9. A workplace in which workers who join the union pay union dues and those who do not join the union pay a fee to the union is a
   A. union shop.
   B. open shop.
   C. closed shop.
   D. semi-union shop.

_____ 10. All of the following are legal ways an employer can discourage unions except
   A. increase worker satisfaction with fair wages and safe working conditions.
   B. enforce a lockout.
   C. discipline union sympathizers.
   D. prolong collective bargaining to discredit the union.

_____ 11. In recent years there has been a trend for unions and employers to cooperate because
   A. trained and experienced workers are an asset.
   B. employees can demand better wages and conditions if the company is successful.
   C. increased productivity tends to save jobs.
   D. all of these

Activity 1 • Analyzing Business News

Directions: Locate a recent newspaper or magazine article that discusses some aspect of unions and labor relations. Provide the article information and answer the questions that follow. If possible, attach the article or a copy of it to this sheet.

Title of article _____

Author _____

Source of article _____

Date _____

1. Topic area (labor law, labor history, collective bargaining, unions, strikes, unions in foreign countries, other)

   _____

2. Is the source of the article a reliable source? Explain why or why not.

   _____

   _____

   _____

3. Write a two- or three-sentence summary of the main facts of the article.

   _____

   _____

   _____

   _____

   _____

4. How might this information benefit or hurt the union movement?

   _____

   _____

   _____

   _____

5. What businesses are affected by this information?

   _____

   _____

6. If you wanted to find additional information about this topic, what key words would you use to search the Internet?

   _____

   _____

7. What additional questions do you have about this topic?

   _____

   _____

   _____

   _____

 ©South-Western Educational Publishing

Chapter 14 OUTLINE
Information Needs for Global Business Activities

GLOBAL FOCUS: ISIS LTD DESIGNS MAJOR INFORMATION SYSTEMS

LESSON 14-1 CREATING GLOBAL INFORMATION SYSTEMS

INFORMATION IS POWER

Strategic Resource

Competitive Advantage

INFORMATION SYSTEMS IN DOMESTIC BUSINESS

INFORMATION SYSTEMS IN INTERNATIONAL BUSINESS

INFORMATION SYSTEM COMPONENTS

DATA INPUTS

OPERATIONAL COMPONENTS

Systems Controls

Database Management

User Interface Systems

Application Systems

Reporting Systems

SYSTEM OUTPUTS

PLANNING AND DEVELOPING THE SYSTEM

ROLE OF TOP-LEVEL MANAGERS

ROLE OF OTHER INFORMATION SYSTEMS MANAGERS

LESSON FEATURES
GLOBAL BUSINESS EXAMPLE: COMPANY EMPLOYEES GETTING WIRED

COMMUNICATION ACROSS BORDERS: THE EVAPORATING E-MAIL MESSAGE

REGIONAL PERSPECTIVE: CULTURE: THE TEMPLES OF ABU SIMBEL

LESSON 14-2 GLOBAL INFORMATION SYSTEMS CHALLENGES

CULTURAL AND COUNTRY ISSUES

LANGUAGE DIFFERENCES

ATTITUDES

BUSINESS AND FINANCIAL ENVIRONMENT

DIFFERING INFORMATION NEEDS

DEGREE OF CONTROL

DATA COLLECTION ISSUES

SOURCES OF DATA

QUALITY OF DATA

Data Validity

Data Reliability

Data Comparability

TECHNOLOGICAL ISSUES

COMMUNICATION TECHNOLOGY

HOST-COUNTRY REQUIREMENTS

HOST-COUNTRY AND INTERNATIONAL REGULATIONS

LESSON FEATURES
A QUESTION OF ETHICS: WHERE DO PERSONAL PRIVACY RIGHTS BEGIN?

GLOBAL BUSINESS EXAMPLE: POTHOLES ALONG THE INFORMATION SUPERHIGHWAY

 ©South-Western Educational Publishing

Lesson 14-1
Creating Global Information Systems

LESSON QUIZ

Directions: For each of the following statements, if the statement is true, write a T on the answer line; if the statement is false, write an F on the answer line.

_____ 1. An extensive information system can give a business a competitive advantage over competitors.

_____ 2. Information systems are the same in domestic and international businesses.

_____ 3. The two kinds of data inputs in an information system are internal organization inputs and external environment inputs.

_____ 4. Statistical analysis and forecasting are examples of application systems.

_____ 5. System outputs consist of the data put into an information system.

_____ 6. Product management outputs in an information system are important because they help managers share information more effectively.

_____ 7. Top-level managers should be involved in planning global information systems because they contribute a vision of the organizational future and can support the development of the system so that the whole organization understands its value.

_____ 8. A global information system usually evolves over time and requires continual maintenance and refinement.

Directions: For each of the following items, decide which choice best completes the statement. Write the letter that identifies your choice on the answer line.

_____ 9. External data inputs include all of the following except
A. market research.
B. economic trends.
C. inventory records.
D. information about competitors.

_____ 10. A global information system must be designed so that it
A. operates for all the languages in the countries involved.
B. considers cultural differences.
C. adjusts to different currencies.
D. all of these

_____ 11. Operational components of an information system include
A. database management, user interface systems, application systems, and reporting systems.
B. product management, communication, sales management, and senior management outputs.
C. data inputs, data outputs, and icons.
D. all of these

Activity 1 • Identifying Internal and External Data Sources

Directions: Read the following scenario. Then, identify whether each item that appears in the list is from an internal data source or an external data source by placing a check mark in the appropriate column.

Scenario: Squeaky Clean is an international distributor featuring environmentally safe cosmetics and personal hygiene products. You have been hired to manage one of its stores in Mexico. As part of the market analysis, you have been asked to identify some internal and external data sources that may provide information that will affect the success of the store. Look at the list of items below and identify which data are from internal sources and which are from external sources.

	Data	From Internal Source	From External Source
1.	Property values		
2.	Age of customers		
3.	Busiest hours		
4.	Currency exchange rates		
5.	Annual reports of competitors		
6.	Employee records		
7.	Interest rates		
8.	Inventory of Squeaky Clean products		
9.	Delivery schedules		
10.	Customer attitudes		

Activity 2 • Analyzing Uses of Information System Outputs

Directions: For the following information system output, describe what kinds of information would be included and how they would be used.

11. Sales budget

Information included: _____

_____

_____

_____

_____

Use of the information: _____

_____

_____

_____

_____

_____

©South-Western Educational Publishing

Lesson 14-2
Global Information Systems Challenges

LESSON QUIZ

Directions: For each of the following statements, if the statement is true, write a T on the answer line; if the statement is false, write an F on the answer line.

_____ 1. Language differences between different countries do not create a problem for a global information system as long as the languages are translated correctly.

_____ 2. Obtaining information from workers in other countries about the effectiveness of a company's management may be difficult due to cultural attitudes toward criticizing authority.

_____ 3. Managers in different countries all need the same financial statements so an information system only needs to provide one set of the statements for each manager.

_____ 4. Secondary data are data that are collected by the user for a specific purpose.

_____ 5. When one country measures a wheat crop by the truckload and another country measures the wheat crop by the ton, data comparability exists.

_____ 6. Data that is gathered must be valid, reliable, and comparable to achieve a high degree of certainty in the system outputs.

_____ 7. Technology issues are generally not a concern if a company has total control over the process.

_____ 8. Differing attitudes toward privacy rights can affect the quality of data gathered.

Directions: For each of the following items, decide which choice best completes the statement. Write the letter that identifies your choice on the answer line.

_____ 9. The information needs of an international business can be different in different locations because
   A. the countries may have different tax systems.
   B. currency exchange rates may fluctuate.
   C. governments may regulate international businesses in different ways.
   D. all of these

_____ 10. One branch manager uses informal interviews with selected customers and another branch manager uses a written questionnaire to gather data about customer satisfaction. The data gathered by the two managers
   A. probably does not pass the test of data reliability.
   B. probably does not pass the test of data validity.
   C. probably does not pass the test of data comparability.
   D. none of these

_____ 11. When a host country does not have sufficient technological infrastructure to support a global information system
   A. a technology issue is involved.
   B. a company may have to transmit less information to that country.
   C. a company may have to transmit information to that country more slowly.
   D. all of these

Activity 1 • Analyzing Uses for Technology

Directions: For each of the following items, identify how an international businessperson can use that technology.

1. Personal Computer _____

_____

2. Voice Synthesizer _____

_____

3. Notebook or Laptop Computer _____

_____

4. Integrated Software _____

_____

5. Desktop Publishing _____

_____

6. E-mail _____

_____

7. Teleconferencing _____

_____

8. The Internet _____

_____

Activity 2 • Determining Research Methods for Gathering Data

Directions: For each of the following items, identify how a company could obtain the data needed.

9. Exchange rates for various currencies _____

_____

10. Area in which retail customers for a store live _____

_____

11. Number of married couples with children _____

_____

12. Number of senior citizens _____

_____

13. Number of cars in the country _____

_____

14. Literacy rate _____

_____

©South-Western Educational Publishing Chapter 14

Chapter 15 OUTLINE
Production Systems for Global Business

GLOBAL FOCUS: MAURITANIA'S RICHES FROM THE SEA

LESSON 15-1 GLOBAL PRODUCTION METHODS

THE PRODUCTION PROCESS

RESOURCES

Natural Resources

Human Resources

Capital Resources

TRANSFORMATION

GOODS AND SERVICES

METHODS OF OPERATIONS MANAGEMENT

Forecasting

Scheduling

Inventory Control

PRODUCTION METHODS AROUND THE WORLD

MANUAL PRODUCTION SYSTEMS

AUTOMATED PRODUCTION SYSTEMS

COMPUTERIZED PRODUCTION SYSTEMS

 ©South-Western Educational Publishing

Computer-Assisted Manufacturing

Robotics

Automated Warehouses

Computer-Integrated Manufacturing

LESSON FEATURES
GLOBAL BUSINESS EXAMPLE: HORIZONTAL AND VERTICAL COMPANIES

COMMUNICATION ACROSS BORDERS: TURNING A DEAF EAR TOWARD TECHNOLOGY

LESSON 15-2 EXPANDING PRODUCTIVE ACTIVITIES

MEASURING PRODUCTION OUTPUT

PRODUCTIVITY

QUALITY CONTROL

Total Quality Control (TQC)

Working in Teams

CREATING AND DELIVERING SERVICES

INFORMATION AND OFFICE PRODUCTION

LESSON FEATURES
GLOBAL BUSINESS EXAMPLE: YOUR CAR IS FROM WHAT COUNTRY?

E-COMMERCE IN ACTION: INTERNATIONAL E-COMMERCE: MASS CUSTOMIZATION

REGIONAL PERSPECTIVE: HISTORY: AN AFRICAN-AMERICAN OIL ENTREPRENEUR

©South-Western Educational Publishing

Lesson 15-1
Global Production Methods

LESSON QUIZ

Directions: For each of the following statements, if the statement is true, write a T on the answer line; if the statement is false, write an F on the answer line.

_____ 1. When raw materials are transformed into finished products they are called resources.

_____ 2. A country's monetary system, tax structure, economic conditions, and availability of materials affect the capital resources of a company.

_____ 3. Transformation occurs only when machines are used to turn resources into finished goods.

_____ 4. Just-in-time (JIT) systems maintain very low inventory.

_____ 5. Forecasting is often based on previous sales figures.

_____ 6. In manual production, robots perform human-like tasks.

_____ 7. In some cases, manual production is necessary because machines cannot do the work and in other cases machines are necessary because people cannot do the work.

_____ 8. It is safer and more efficient to have humans, rather than robots, perform very repetitious or very dangerous tasks.

_____ 9. Manual production is still used in many parts of the world—especially in less developed countries.

Directions: For each of the following items, decide which choice best completes the statement. Write the letter that identifies your choice on the answer line.

_____ 10. The major elements of the production process are
  A. natural resources, human resources, and capital resources.
  B. forecasting, scheduling, and inventory control.
  C. resources, transformation, and final goods and services.
  D. none of these

_____ 11. Many developing countries must continue to use manual production systems because
  A. handmade items are considered more valuable than machine-made items.
  B. machines would replace workers and lead to high unemployment.
  C. it was the earliest means of production.
  D. they may not be able to afford the initial cost of machinery.

_____ 12. The manufacturing system in which computers are used to run production equipment is called
  A. computer-assisted manufacturing (CAM).
  B. robotics.
  C. automated warehouses.
  D. computer-integrated manufacturing (CIM).

Activity 1 • Identifying Stages of Production

Directions: For each of the following activities, use a check mark to identify whether the good or activity is a resource, transformation process, or finished good.

		Resource	Transformation Process	Finished Good
1.	Gold bars are distributed to banks.			
2.	Gold ore is discovered in mines.			
3.	A partner in the venture provides capital to dig a new mine.			
4.	Ore is processed to separate gold from other materials.			
5.	Gold necklaces and rings are displayed in shop windows.			
6.	Gold undergoes a smelting process to achieve the highest purity.			

Activity 2 • Identifying Examples of Resources and Production

Directions: For each of the following items, create an example of the term listed. Use examples from your own knowledge, experience, or imagination.

7. natural resource: _____

_____

8. human resource: _____

_____

9. capital resource: _____

_____

10. transformation activity: _____

_____

11. manual production: _____

_____

12. just-in-time (JIT): _____

_____

13. robotics: _____

_____

14. service industry: _____

_____

©South-Western Educational Publishing

Lesson 15-2
Expanding Productive Activities

LESSON QUIZ

Directions: For each of the following statements, if the statement is true, write a T on the answer line; if the statement is false, write an F on the answer line.

_____ 1. The two measures of production output are productivity and quality control.

_____ 2. Industries establish standards for their products to maintain quality control.

_____ 3. The total quality control approach requires that only managers and supervisors be responsible for high-quality production.

_____ 4. A quality circle is a round seal placed on goods that have been inspected by quality control.

_____ 5. People working in teams need to safeguard and emphasize their own individual accomplishments to be successful.

_____ 6. The main advantage of a cross-functional team approach to problem-solving is that multiple points of view are brought to solving the problem.

_____ 7. A grocery store that provides stations at which customers scan and pay for their own groceries is using tailored logistics.

_____ 8. A notebook computer is an example of an office machine that is smaller, faster, and more connected than previous products that performed similar functions.

Directions: For each of the following items, decide which choice best completes the statement. Write the letter that identifies your choice on the answer line.

_____ 9. The amount of work that is accomplished in a unit of time is called
   A. quality control.
   B. quality circle.
   C. productivity.
   D. synchronized manufacturing.

_____ 10. Productivity can be increased by
   A. replacing an older, slower machine with a newer, faster one.
   B. using just-in-time inventory control.
   C. distributing the workflow as needed throughout the production cycle.
   D. all of these

_____ 11. The process of measuring goods and services against a product standard is called
   A. productivity.
   B. synchronized manufacturing.
   C. quality control.
   D. a cross-functional team.

Activity 1 • Analyzing Industry Output
Directions: Use the following table to answer the questions that follow.

U.S. NATIONAL INCOME
FROM PRIVATE DOMESTIC INDUSTRIES (PDIs)

Private Domestic Industries	1960 (Billions of Dollars)	Percentage of Total PDIs	1998 (Billions of Dollars)	Percentage of Total PDIs
Agriculture, forestry, fisheries	$17.8	4.8%	$104.2	1.7%
Mining	5.6	1.5%	50.6	0.8%
Construction	22.5	6.1%	331.1	5.5%
Manufacturing	125.3	33.7%	1,168.7	19.3%
Transportation, public utilities	35.8	9.6%	500.8	8.3%
Wholesale trade	25.0	6.7%	409.2	6.8%
Retail trade	41.3	11.1%	580.0	9.6%
Finance, insurance, real estate	51.3	13.8%	1,273.5	21.1%
Services	46.9	12.6%	1,624.9	26.9%
Total	$371.5	100.0%*	$6,043.0	100.0%

Sum may not equal 100.0% due to rounding.

1. By how many dollars did income by private industries increase from 1960 to 1998? _____

2. Which industry made up the largest percentage of the private domestic income in 1960? _____

3. Which industry made up the smallest percentage of the private domestic income in 1960? _____

4. Which industry made up the largest percentage of the private domestic income in 1998? _____

5. Which industry made up the smallest percentage of the private domestic income in 1998? _____

6. Which industries grew in their percentage of the private domestic income between 1960 and 1998? ____

7. Which industries decreased in their percentage of the private domestic income between 1960 and 1998?

8. Which industry had the largest growth in percentage of the private domestic income between 1960 and 1998? _____

9. Which industry lost the greatest percentage of the private domestic income between 1960 and 1998? ___

©South-Western Educational Publishing Chapter 15

Chapter 16 OUTLINE
Global Marketing and Consumer Behavior

GLOBAL FOCUS: BREAKFAST IN BRITAIN

LESSON 16-1 MARKETING AROUND THE WORLD

INTERNATIONAL MARKETS

CONSUMER MARKETS

ORGANIZATIONAL MARKETS

GLOBAL MARKETING OPPORTUNITIES

EXPANDED COMMUNICATIONS

TECHNOLOGY

CHANGING POLITICAL SITUATIONS

INCREASED COMPETITION

CHANGING DEMOGRAPHICS

LESSON FEATURES
GLOBAL BUSINESS EXAMPLE: GLOBAL MARKETING OF FAST FOOD

REGIONAL PERSPECTIVE: GEOGRAPHY: THE RAIN FOREST

LESSON 16-2 THE MARKETING MIX AND THE MARKETING PLAN

THE MARKETING MIX

PRODUCT

PRICE

DISTRIBUTION

PROMOTION

MARKETING OF SERVICES

THE MARKETING PLAN

Company Goals

Description of Customers and Their Needs

Competitors

Economic, Social, Legal, and Technological Trends

Financial and Human Resources

Time Line

Methods of Measuring Success

ELEMENTS OF AN INTERNATIONAL MARKETING PLAN

LESSON FEATURE
E-COMMERCE IN ACTION: JAPANESE CONVENIENCE STORES GO ONLINE

LESSON 16-3 PLANNING GLOBAL MARKETING ACTIVITIES

THE MARKETING ENVIRONMENT

Geography

Economic Conditions

Social and Cultural Influences

Political and Legal Factors

CONSUMER BEHAVIOR

PHYSICAL AND EMOTIONAL NEEDS

GEOGRAPHIC AND DEMOGRAPHIC NEEDS

PERSONALITY AND PSYCHOGRAPHIC FACTORS

SOCIAL AND CULTURAL FACTORS

SELECTING A TARGET MARKET

MARKET SEGMENTS

TARGET MARKET

LESSON FEATURES
A QUESTION OF ETHICS: SELLING LUXURY ITEMS IN LESS DEVELOPED ECONOMIES

GLOBAL BUSINESS EXAMPLE: MARKET SEGMENTS OF THE RUSSIAN CONSUMER

©South-Western Educational Publishing

Lesson 16-1
Marketing Around the World

LESSON QUIZ

Directions: For each of the following statements, if the statement is true, write a T on the answer line; if the statement is false, write an F on the answer line.

_____ 1. Production is an example of a marketing activity.

_____ 2. A market consists of the likely customers for a good or service in a certain geographic location.

_____ 3. Individual buyers of goods and services are commonly called commercial markets.

_____ 4. Businesses often expand into other countries to develop new markets to maintain and expand profits.

_____ 5. Computer networks, the Internet, video teleconferencing, and other advances in communications systems have had little impact on international business.

_____ 6. Automated production systems usually make it more difficult for a company to set up a manufacturing plant in another country.

_____ 7. Several countries that used to have communist governments are interested in new trading partners in other parts of the world in order to achieve economic growth.

_____ 8. A person's age and income are examples of demographic data.

_____ 9. The first step in the marketing process is to plan the marketing strategy.

Directions: For each of the following items, decide which choice best completes the statement. Write the letter that identifies your choice on the answer line.

_____ 10. Marketing activities include
   A. scheduling, planning, and evaluating success.
   B. shipping, pricing, and advertising.
   C. demographics, transformation, and advertising.
   D. none of these

_____ 11. An example of a consumer market is
   A. people who like to buy expensive sports cars.
   B. people who want to rent office space to start a business.
   C. wholesalers who purchase goods to resell to retailers.
   D. companies that purchase parts for making radios.

_____ 12. All of the following are examples of demographic characteristics except
   A. the literacy rate of a country.
   B. the average life expectancy of the population of a country.
   C. the form of government of a country.
   D. the number, size, and kinds of occupational groups in a country.

Activity 1 • Identifying Consumer and Commercial Markets

Directions: For each of the following marketing situations, use a check mark to indicate whether it is an example of a consumer or a commercial market.

		Consumer	Commercial
1.	A hospital in France purchases bedding from a Colombian company.		
2.	A computer company in Brazil buys automobiles for use by its repair staff.		
3.	A family in Panama buys an automobile.		
4.	An exporting company buys a computer to keep inventory records.		
5.	A person from Canada takes a vacation in Argentina.		
6.	A business owner who operates a company from her home buys a fax machine to receive orders.		

Activity 2 • Identifying Market Opportunities Using Demographics

Directions: For each of the following demographic characteristics, describe at least two different products and/or services that could be new market opportunities.

7. The average life expectancy in this country has increased so that there is now a large population of people over 65 years old.

_____

_____

_____

8. In this country many more women are rapidly obtaining management-level jobs.

_____

_____

_____

9. In this country there was a sharp rise in the birthrate 12 years ago.

_____

_____

_____

10. This country's soccer team has won the international matches two years in a row and the team members are considered national heroes and are greatly admired and imitated.

_____

_____

_____

11. The average number of hours worked by employees has dropped from 40 to 34 in recent years in this country.

_____

_____

Lesson 16-2
The Marketing Mix and the Marketing Plan

LESSON QUIZ

Directions: For each of the following statements, if the statement is true, write a T on the answer line; if the statement is false, write an F on the answer line.

_____ 1. The marketing mix consists of product, price, distribution, and promotion.

_____ 2. Transporting, storing, and sorting are part of the promotion component of the marketing mix.

_____ 3. Advertising, pricing, and distribution of services are the same for the marketing of goods.

_____ 4. A marketing plan describes the marketing activities of an organization.

_____ 5. Failing to meet the time line of a marketing plan can result in a marketing failure.

_____ 6. After the marketing plan is completed, the human resources department must determine whether there are sufficient human resources to fulfill the marketing plan.

_____ 7. A product is usually sold at the same price everywhere in the world, although the price is converted to the local currency.

_____ 8. The infrastructure of a country can affect the marketing plan.

_____ 9. Usually, advertising for a product can be the same in every country as long as the language is changed.

Directions: For each of the following items, decide which choice best completes the statement. Write the letter that identifies your choice on the answer line.

_____ 10. In the marketing mix, the element of product involves all of the following considerations except
   A. whether the product is a good or a service.
   B. how local customs or attitudes affect the popularity of the product.
   C. how the product will be shipped to the customer.
   D. whether the product can be sold in a standardized form or will need to be adapted to local situations.

_____ 11. In the marketing mix, the element of distribution involves all of the following considerations except
   A. where the product will be stored prior to shipping to another country.
   B. how the retailer will display the product after it is received from the wholesaler.
   C. how to send products ordered from the company's web site on the Internet.
   D. whether to sell the product directly to wholesalers, retailers, or consumers.

_____ 12. The marketing of services is usually similar to the marketing of goods except for
   A. price.
   B. distribution.
   C. promotion.
   D. technological trends.

Activity 1 • Analyzing Marketing Mix Components in an Advertisement

Directions: Select a magazine advertisement or television commercial. Based on your analysis of the ad, describe what the company is doing for each component of the marketing mix.

1. Product (or service) _____

2. Company name _____

3. Source of advertisement _____

4. Date of advertisement _____

5. Product _____

6. Price _____

7. Distribution _____

_____

8. Promotion _____

_____

Activity 2 • Analyzing Marketing Mix Components

Directions: Assume that you are responsible for writing the marketing plan for a product that will be marketed to the students in your class. Choose a product and write brief statements to complete the following marketing plan for the product.

9. Product (or service) _____

_____

10. Company goals _____

_____

11. Customers and their needs _____

_____

12. Competitors _____

_____

_____

13. Economic, social, legal, and technological trends _____

_____

_____

14. Financial and human resources _____

_____

_____

15. Time line _____

_____

_____

16. Methods for measuring success _____

_____

_____

 ©South-Western Educational Publishing

Lesson 16-3
Planning Global Marketing Activities

LESSON QUIZ

Directions: For each of the following statements, if the statement is true, write a T on the answer line; if the statement is false, write an F on the answer line.

_____ 1. Food is a physical need that influences consumer behavior.

_____ 2. Consumer demand can be affected by high inflation.

_____ 3. Consumer behavior is really quite complex and involves several factors.

_____ 4. Consumers in different countries may have different personality and psychographic factors, but consumer physical and emotional needs are the same in all countries.

_____ 5. Social experiences can result in different consumer psychographics from country to country.

_____ 6. Psychographics involve consumer behavior factors based on population characteristics.

_____ 7. A market segment is the price a company charges for its product.

_____ 8. A company frequently defines a target market for its products and then attempts to meet the specific needs of the customers in that target market.

Directions: For each of the following items, decide which choice best completes the statement. Write the letter that identifies your choice on the answer line.

_____ 9. The four factors that make up the marketing environment are
   A. product, price, distribution, and promotion.
   B. psychographics, demographics, consumer behavior, and market segments.
   C. geography, economic conditions, social and cultural influences, and political and legal factors.
   D. none of these

_____ 10. Economic conditions in a country can affect a product's
   A. selling price.
   B. consumer demand.
   C. profits.
   D. all of these

_____ 11. A person's psychographic profile may include information about
   A. food preferences, age, gender, and education level.
   B. hobbies, family activities, work interests, and social opinions.
   C. political opinions, attitudes about risk and change, and climate.
   D. none of these

_____ 12. A market segment can be defined by
   A. psychographics and demographics.
   B. hobbies, family activities, work interests, or social opinions.
   C. product benefits.
   D. all of these

Activity 1 • Identifying Consumer Behavior Influences

Directions: For each of the following needs or factors that affect consumer behavior, describe a product or service that could fulfill that need. Student answers will vary.

1. Physical and emotional needs _____

_____

_____

2. Geographic and demographic factors _____

_____

_____

3. Personality and psychographic factors _____

_____

_____

4. Social and cultural factors _____

_____

_____

Activity 2 • Identifying Market Segments

Directions: For each of the following situations, place the correct letter(s) in the space provided for the type of market segment activity described.

A. Demographic segmentation
B. Psychographic segmentation
C. Buying behavior segmentation
D. Product benefit segmentation

_____ 5. Customers in one country think taste is the most important aspect of a food product; customers in another country are looking for the lowest cost of the item.

_____ 6. Consumers with young children are told about a store with a play center for youngsters.

_____ 7. People who believe that the environment is important see a commercial about a company's recycling efforts.

_____ 8. Some people prefer a home computer with many uses; others want a computer that is fast.

_____ 9. A new product is planned that will appeal to single people.

_____10. As more people have home computers, companies are planning to advertise through an online service.

_____11. The health concerns of customers have made a food company revise the ingredients of its products.

_____12. Retired people usually have more time to travel; a vacation service company is planning ads aimed at older consumers.

_____13. A U.S. fast-food company changes its menu in a foreign country because some food items are prohibited by religious beliefs.

_____14. A company that manufactures microwave cookware advertises in airline magazines to appeal to the female business traveler.

 ©South-Western Educational Publishing

Chapter 17 OUTLINE
Developing Goods and Services for Global Markets

GLOBAL FOCUS: GLOBAL STRATEGY FOR BARBIE

LESSON 17-1 GLOBAL PRODUCT PLANNING

INTERNATIONAL PRODUCT OPPORTUNITIES

New Product

Improved Product

Existing Product with a New Use

Existing Product Sold in a New Market

MARKETING PRODUCTS AROUND THE WORLD

CONSUMER PRODUCT CATEGORIES

Convenience Goods

Shopping Goods

Specialty Goods

THE PRODUCT LINE

ORGANIZATIONAL PRODUCTS

CONSUMER SERVICES

CHARACTERISTICS OF SERVICES

TYPES OF SERVICES

Rented-goods Services

Owned-goods Services

Non-goods Services

©South-Western Educational Publishing

MARKETING OF SERVICES

SERVICES AND INTERNATIONAL TRADE

LESSON FEATURES
GLOBAL BUSINESS EXAMPLE: A JAPANESE APPROACH FOR PRODUCT DEVELOPMENT

COMMUNICATION ACROSS BORDERS: COMMUNICATE WITH CUSTOMERS IN THEIR OWN LANGUAGE

LESSON 17-2 DEVELOPING AND RESEARCHING PRODUCTS

CREATING NEW PRODUCTS

NEW PRODUCTS

Customer Needs

Technology

NEW PRODUCT DEVELOPMENT PROCESS

Generating Product Ideas

Evaluating Product Ideas

Researching Product Ideas

Marketing Product Ideas

ADAPTING PRODUCTS TO FOREIGN MARKETS

THE MARKETING RESEARCH PROCESS

DATA COLLECTION AND ANALYSIS FOR MARKETING RESEARCH

SECONDARY DATA

PRIMARY DATA

Surveys

Observations

Experiments

ANALYZING AND USING RESEARCH DATA

LESSON FEATURE
GLOBAL BUSINESS EXAMPLE: COLLECTING MARKETING RESEARCH DATA IN VENEZUELA

LESSON 17-3 AN INTERNATIONAL PRODUCT STRATEGY

BRANDING AND PACKAGING

BRANDING AND MARKETING

TYPES OF BRANDS

PACKAGING

PLANNING A GLOBAL PRODUCT STRATEGY

THE PRODUCT LIFE CYCLE

Introduction

Growth

Maturity

Decline

GLOBAL PRODUCT DECISIONS

CEASING FOREIGN MARKET ACTIVITIES

LESSON FEATURES
GLOBAL BUSINESS EXAMPLE: THE WORLD'S MOST FAMOUS BRANDS

E-COMMERCE IN ACTION: E-BRANDS

REGIONAL PERSPECTIVE: CULTURE: THE GAUCHOS OF ARGENTINA

Lesson 17-1
Global Product Planning

LESSON QUIZ

Directions: For each of the following statements, if the statement is true, write a T on the answer line; if the statement is false, write an F on the answer line.

_____ 1. A convenience good is usually purchased after consumers compare brands and stores.

_____ 2. A product line consists of inexpensive items that require little shopping effort.

_____ 3. A product that is a convenience good in one country could be a shopping good in another country.

_____ 4. A marketing effort that communicates differences in price, quality, and features of various brands is appropriate for shopping goods.

_____ 5. Packaged frozen foods that include vegetables, desserts, entrees, and complete meals are an example of a product line.

_____ 6. Organizational products usually require some adaptation for a foreign market.

_____ 7. A hotel room is an example of a non-goods service.

_____ 8. Services are intangible products available for sale by a company.

_____ 9. In the United States, more people work in service industries than in manufacturing industries.

Directions: For each of the following items, decide which choice best completes the statement. Write the letter that identifies your choice on the answer line.

_____10. The marketing goal of satisfying needs that have not been met can be achieved in all of the following ways except
A. by selling the product in a country in which it has never been sold before.
B. by adding a new variation to an existing product.
C. by changing the price of a product.
D. by promoting a new use for an existing product.

_____11. A personal computer for home use is
A. a convenience good.
B. a shopping good.
C. a specialty good.
D. an intangible good.

_____12. All of the following are examples of the special marketing efforts required for services except
A. convenience of location.
B. the business's image.
C. the uniformity of the product.
D. the clothing or uniforms worn by employees.

Activity 1 • Identifying Types of Consumer Products

Directions: For each of the following goods, write the letter that identifies the type of product on the answer line.

A. Convenience good
B. Shopping good
C. Specialty good

_____ 1. Shoes by a famous designer

_____ 2. Watch with diamonds

_____ 3. Bread

_____ 4. Video games

_____ 5. Juice drink

_____ 6. Newspaper

_____ 7. Computer software

_____ 8. Sweater

Activity 2 • Analyzing the Marketing of a Service

Directions: Select a service that you or a family member uses. The service should be one that you have to go to the office of the service provider to receive. Then provide the following information about that service.

9. What is the service? _____

10. What is the name of the business that provides the service? _____

11. What is the address of the service? _____

12. How many locations does this business have? Why is that important? _____
_____

13. How did you select this business to provide that service? _____
_____

14. What is your overall impression of the business? _____

15. Describe what the place of business looks like. _____
_____

16. Describe how the people who work at the business dress. _____
_____

17. How does the appearance of the business and its employees affect the business? _____
_____

18. Is the service provided to you by this business exactly the same as the service provided to other customers? Describe any similarities or differences. _____
_____

19. What changes would you recommend to this business to be more successful? _____
_____

Lesson 17-2
Developing and Researching Products

LESSON QUIZ

Directions: For each of the following statements, if the statement is true, write a T on the answer line; if the statement is false, write an F on the answer line.

_____ 1. Technology can make new products available to meet consumer needs and wants.

_____ 2. The four steps in the marketing research process are identify the problem, collect data, analyze the data, and launch the new product.

_____ 3. Secondary data are widely available in all countries.

_____ 4. Primary data are always a better source of marketing information than secondary data.

_____ 5. Marketing reports in a company library are examples of secondary data.

_____ 6. Focus groups are commonly used to collect data for quantitative research studies.

_____ 7. Focus groups and personal interviews might not provide useful information in some cultures.

_____ 8. Observational research allows a company to gather data about consumer attitudes and opinions.

_____ 9. A test market is a type of experimental research.

Directions: For each of the following items, decide which choice best completes the statement. Write the letter that identifies your choice on the answer line.

_____ 10. Companies produce new products for all of the following reasons except
   A. old products become unpopular with customers.
   B. competitors enter the market and attract customers.
   C. sales decline because the product becomes obsolete.
   D. all of these

_____ 11. In the second step in the new-product development process, evaluating product ideas,
   A. marketing research is conducted to measure customer attitudes and potential sales.
   B. new technology is examined to determine whether new products can be created.
   C. managers determine whether the new product can be sold at an acceptable price.
   D. none of these

_____ 12. A research method that measures consumer behavior is
   A. conducting a survey or interview.
   B. holding a focus group session.
   C. referring to computerized databases.
   D. observational research.

_____ 13. An example of secondary data is
   A. a test market.
   B. a focus group.
   C. a survey using a written questionnaire sent by mail.
   D. a government database.

Activity 1 • Identifying Examples of Sources of New Products
Directions: For each of the following sources of new products, create an example of a recently introduced product or one that might be successful.

1. Technology _____

_____

_____

2. Consumer needs _____

_____

_____

3. Changing demographics _____

_____

_____

Activity 2 • Creating an Example of the Marketing Research Process
Directions: For each step of the marketing research process, create an example of actions a company might take for a research study in another country.

4. Phase 1: Identify problem _____

_____

5. Phase 2: Collect data _____

_____

6. Phase 3: Analyze data _____

_____

7. Phase 4: Report results _____

_____

Activity 3 • Identifying International Marketing Research Information
Directions: For each of the following, use a check mark to indicate whether the item is an example of secondary or primary data.

		Secondary Data	Primary Data
8.	A survey a company will conduct in Poland to determine video viewing habits		
9.	A report published by the government of Italy listing the number of children in households with different incomes		
10.	An available computerized database of export data		
11.	A published report of a multinational company comparing sales results of its products in different geographic regions		
12.	An observational research study to be conducted to measure buying behaviors of parents shopping with children		

Lesson 17-3
An International Product Strategy

LESSON QUIZ

Directions: For each of the following statements, if the statement is true, write a T on the answer line; if the statement is false, write an F on the answer line.

_____ 1. It is common to use a brand for a product that is a good, but it isn't possible to give a service a brand name.

_____ 2. A global brand is used on products sold in many countries.

_____ 3. A national brand is a brand name that is well known within one country.

_____ 4. Sometimes a national brand can become a global brand.

_____ 5. Government regulation can restrict what appears on the package of a product.

_____ 6. Companies are usually more concerned with making the package of a product easy to use than they are with capturing the attention of customers.

_____ 7. Competition is most intense in the introduction stage of the product life cycle.

_____ 8. Most products can expect a product life cycle of several years or more, but electronic products frequently have a life cycle that can be measured in months.

_____ 9. Companies frequently discontinue a product when sales continue to decline in order to focus on more profitable products.

Directions: For each of the following items, decide which choice best completes the statement. Write the letter that identifies your choice on the answer line.

_____10. A product that has no brand name, usually comes in a plain package or wrapper, and is often sold for less than a name brand product is a
   A. regional brand.
   B. store brand.
   C. manufacturer's brand.
   D. generic.

_____11. Kodak and Sony are examples of
   A. global brands.
   B. national brands.
   C. manufacturer's brands.
   D. generics.

_____12. The stage of the product life cycle in which the product has few competitors and marketing activities should create consumer awareness is the
   A. introduction stage.
   B. growth stage.
   C. decline stage.
   D. none of these

Activity 1 • Analyzing the Stages of the Product Life Cycle

Directions: For each stage of the product life cycle (1) list a product that you believe is in that stage and (2) explain in the space provided why you believe the item is in that stage.

1. Product

Introduction	Growth	Maturity	Decline

2. Explanation

a. Introduction _____

_____

_____

_____

b. Growth _____

_____

_____

c. Maturity _____

_____

_____

d. Decline _____

_____

_____

Activity 2 • Analyzing Product Packaging

Directions: Think about a common product that you or a family member has purchased at a grocery or discount store. Then describe how the package for that product functions in each of the following areas.

3. Name and brand of product _____

4. Protects the product _____

_____

5. Captures the customer's attention _____

_____

_____

6. Is sensitive to environmental concerns _____

_____

7. Meets government regulations _____

_____

 ©South-Western Educational Publishing

Chapter 18 OUTLINE
Global Pricing and Distribution Strategies

GLOBAL FOCUS: TOYS "R" US IN JAPAN

LESSON 18-1 INTERNATIONAL PRICING ACTIVITIES

PRICE PLANNING FOR INTERNATIONAL MARKETING

COSTS

CONSUMER DEMAND

COMPETITION

PRICE SELECTION METHODS

MARKUP PRICING

NEW PRODUCT PRICING

Competitive Pricing

Skim Pricing

Penetration Pricing

PSYCHOLOGICAL PRICING

Promotional Pricing

Odd-Even Pricing

Prestige Pricing

Price Lining

DISCOUNT PRICING

Seasonal Discounts

Cash Discounts

©South-Western Educational Publishing Chapter 18

Quantity Discounts

Trade Discounts

PRICING IN GLOBAL MARKETS

LESSON FEATURES
GLOBAL BUSINESS EXAMPLE: SKIPPY IN HUNGARY

A QUESTION OF ETHICS: DUMPING

LESSON 18-2 GLOBAL DISTRIBUTION ACTIVITIES

DISTRIBUTION CHANNELS

DISTRIBUTION CHANNEL MEMBERS

AGENTS

WHOLESALERS

RETAILERS

Convenience Stores

General Merchandise Retailers

Specialty Stores

Direct Sellers

Online Retailers

Automatic Vending

INTERNATIONAL RETAILING ACTIVITIES

GLOBAL INTERMEDIARIES

EXPORT MANAGEMENT COMPANY

EXPORT TRADING COMPANY

FREIGHT FORWARDER

CUSTOMS BROKER

©South-Western Educational Publishing

LESSON FEATURES

GLOBAL BUSINESS EXAMPLE: COKE VS. PEPSI AT THE BERLIN WALL

COMMUNICATION ACROSS BORDERS: FLEXIBLE SCHEDULING—BRAZILIAN STYLE

LESSON 18-3 MOVING GOODS AROUND THE WORLD

PREPARING FOR SHIPPING

PACKING AND LABELING

DOCUMENTATION

Bill of Lading

Certificate of Origin

Export Declaration

Destination Control Statement

Insurance Certificate

TRANSPORTATION IN THE GLOBAL MARKET

Motor Carrier

Railroad

Waterway

Pipeline

Air Carrier

Intermodal Movements

LESSON FEATURES
GLOBAL BUSINESS EXAMPLE: AVON IN THE AMAZON

REGIONAL PERSPECTIVE: HISTORY: THE PANAMA CANAL

©South-Western Educational Publishing

Lesson 18-1
International Pricing Activities

LESSON QUIZ

Directions: For each of the following statements, if the statement is true, write a T on the answer line; if the statement is false, write an F on the answer line.

_____ 1. Higher incomes in a country usually result in lower demand and lower prices for products.

_____ 2. As more companies compete in a market, prices tend to rise.

_____ 3. An item that costs a store $60 and has a markup of 100 percent would sell to customers for $120.

_____ 4. Products with an inconsistent demand, such as jewelry, will often have higher markups because the product has higher carrying costs than products that have consistent demand.

_____ 5. When a company wants many customers for its new product, it will usually set a relatively low price.

_____ 6. Odd-even pricing, prestige pricing, and price lining are methods of psychological pricing approaches.

_____ 7. Cash discounts are offered to customers so that sellers do not have to pay credit card companies a percentage of their sales.

_____ 8. Two ways to minimize the effect of fluctuating currency exchange rates when setting prices are to use countertrade and to set prices high enough to offset increasing exchange rates.

_____ 9. Dumping involves selling products in one country at a lower price than in the home company's country.

Directions: For each of the following items, decide which choice best completes the statement. Write the letter that identifies your choice on the answer line.

_____10. The kind of pricing being used when an amount is added to the cost of a product to determine the selling price is
A. skim pricing.
B. markup pricing.
C. promotional pricing.
D. none of these

_____11. Skim pricing occurs when
A. a new product has competition and the price is set at a price similar to the competing products.
B. a new product is introduced and managers set a relatively high introductory price.
C. a new product is introduced at a relatively low price to skim customers from the competitors.
D. a new product is introduced at a price that includes a specific markup percentage over the cost of the product.

_____12. When terms of sale are expressed as 1/10, net 20,
A. customers may deduct one-tenth if they pay within 20 days of the sale.
B. customers may deduct 1 percent if they pay within 20 days of the sale.
C. customers may deduct one-tenth if they pay within 10 days of the sale and must pay the full amount within 20 days.
D. none of these

Activity 1 • Analyzing Factors Affecting Prices

Directions: For each of the following situations, use a check mark to indicate whether prices will be affected by costs, consumer demand, or competition.

		Costs	Consumer Demand	Competition
1.	The price of video rentals has declined as two new stores opened in a geographic area.			
2.	Workers are given an increase in wages.			
3.	Taxes on imported raw materials have been raised.			
4.	Many people want to buy a popular new clothing item.			
5.	Salaries rise in an area, thus making more money available for spending by households.			
6.	A shortage of computer chips causes prices of these chips to rise.			

Activity 2 • Calculating Prices for International Business

Directions: Calculate the price in each of the following international marketing situations.

7. A Mexican store marks up its prices 60 percent. What would be the selling price for a sweater that cost the store $40 (pesos)?

8. A Japanese company offers a 4 percent discount to a customer to pay for a ¥9,000 purchase within 10 days. What amount would the customer pay if paying within 10 days?

9. An Israeli store sells automobile tires for IS65 each if three or fewer are purchased, or IS60 each if a customer buys four or more. What would be the cost of eight tires?

10. A French computer manufacturer sells to retailers with a trade discount of 60 percent. If a notebook computer has a list price to consumers of Fr5,500, what would be the cost of the item to the store?

11. A Danish customer makes a purchase of Kr$1,200 on April 15, with terms of 3/10, net/30. How much should the customer pay on April 22? How much should the customer pay on March 3?

12. Quantity discounts for bags of wheat in Bolivia are: 1-4 bags, B5.50; 5-8 bags, B5.20; 9-10 bags, B5.00; and more than 10 bags, B4.80. What is the cost of 6 bags? 10 bags? 16 bags?

Lesson 18-2
Global Distribution Activities

LESSON QUIZ

Directions: For each of the following statements, if the statement is true, write a T on the answer line; if the statement is false, write an F on the answer line.

_____ 1. An indirect distribution channel uses agents, wholesalers, and/or retailers.

_____ 2. The difference between a direct and an indirect distribution channel is the final user of the product.

_____ 3. Companies use wholesalers to distribute their products to retailers because wholesalers specialize in transporting, storing, and ordering goods.

_____ 4. Retailers are businesses that buy large quantities of an item and resell them to stores.

_____ 5. Mail order and telephone sales are commonly called direct selling.

_____ 6. A vending machine can be considered a retailer.

_____ 7. A form of direct distribution that is expected to increase for many years is online selling.

_____ 8. A freight forwarder provides complete distribution services for businesses that desire to sell in foreign markets.

Directions: For each of the following items, decide which choice best completes the statement. Write the letter that identifies your choice on the answer line.

_____ 9. All of the following are examples of a direct distribution channel except
   A. a company that sells its goods through its web site on the Internet.
   B. a company that sells goods to a wholesaler.
   C. a company that sells its goods in its own retail outlets.
   D. all of these

_____ 10. All of the following are examples of specialty stores except
   A. a jewelry store.
   B. a toy store.
   C. a department store.
   D. a camera store.

_____ 11. All of the following are examples of retailers except
   A. a family sells its own produce at a sidewalk stand in Costa Rica.
   B. a man sells fish he has caught from his boat in the bay in Hong Kong.
   C. a woman sells cosmetic products for a large manufacturer at private theme parties.
   D. a paper manufacturer sells paper to printers for printing books for publishing companies.

_____ 12. A global intermediary that buys and sells products and distributes those goods to markets in other countries is
   A. an export management company.
   B. an export trading company.
   C. a freight forwarder.
   D. a customs broker.

Activity 1 • Analyzing Retailer Services

Directions: Based on a store visit or an analysis of advertisements, describe the following features for a retailer in your area.

1. Store name _____

2. Location _____

3. Product selection _____

_____

_____

_____

4. Convenience _____

_____

_____

_____

5. Product quality _____

_____

_____

_____

6. Sales staff assistance _____

_____

_____

_____

7. Special services _____

_____

_____

_____

Activity 2 • Identifying Global Intermediaries

Directions: Write the identifying letter on the answer line to match the situations to the type of global intermediary that would best meet the needs described.

    A. Export management company

    B. Export trading company

    C. Freight forwarder

    D. Customs broker

_____ 8. A company needs help to get imported goods into a country.

_____ 9. A company needs market research and financing assistance to export electronic parts.

_____10. A small manufacturing company needs toasters shipped to Thailand.

_____11. An exporting company needs information on duties imposed by various countries

_____12. A small company wants to find customers in Argentina for its clothing products.

 ©South-Western Educational Publishing

Lesson 18-3
Moving Goods Around the World

LESSON QUIZ

Directions: For each of the following statements, if the statement is true, write a T on the answer line; if the statement is false, write an F on the answer line.

_____ 1. International shippers recommend that exporters label packages with the brand names and contents.

_____ 2. Symbols instead of words are frequently used on packages being shipped internationally because they are universally recognized.

_____ 3. A bill of lading serves as a receipt for exported items.

_____ 4. An export declaration is required by the U.S. Department of Commerce for a shipment with a value of more than $500.

_____ 5. Motor carriers are a form of shipping that is available in nearly every country and quickly delivers shipments of many sizes to nearly anywhere.

_____ 6. A very slow but cost-effective means of international shipping is oceangoing ships.

_____ 7. Containerization refers to the capability of each seller using containers of all sizes for international shipments.

_____ 8. It is not possible to do international shipments of products that require refrigeration.

_____ 9. Intermodal shipping methods ship goods by transferring them between different kinds of carriers.

Directions: For each of the following items, decide which choice best completes the statement. Write the letter that identifies your choice on the answer line.

_____ 10. A document that accompanies international shipments that shows the country in which the goods being shipped were produced is a
A. bill of lading.
B. certificate of origin.
C. export declaration.
D. destination control statement.

_____ 11. Piggyback operations refer to
A. goods that are shipped in containers and stacked on top of each other.
B. goods that are shipped by railroads because they are stacked on flat cars to cross countries.
C. goods that are shipped over the long haul by railroad and then loaded into trucks for door-to-door delivery.
D. goods that are shipped on the decks of oceangoing ships or inland waterway barges.

_____ 12. All of the following are criteria for packing goods for international shipments except
A. maintaining the company's image.
B. minimizing theft.
C. maintaining the lowest possible weight and volume to minimize shipping costs.
D. providing moisture-proof conditions.

Activity 1 • Selecting Transportation Modes for International Marketing

Directions: For each of the following situations, select the transportation mode you consider most appropriate and write it in the space provided. Then, enter your reason for choosing that mode of transportation.

Transportation Modes
- air carrier
- motor carrier
- pipeline
- railroad
- waterway

1. Shipping oil from an oil field to a seaport for overseas export.

   Transportation mode: _____

   Reason: _____

   _____

   _____

2. Shipping blood to needed areas.

   Transportation mode: _____

   Reason: _____

   _____

   _____

3. Shipping large machinery across the ocean.

   Transportation mode: _____

   Reason: _____

   _____

   _____

4. Shipping farm products to major cities.

   Transportation mode: _____

   Reason: _____

   _____

   _____

5. Shipping delicate computer parts from Asia to Brazil.

   Transportation mode: _____

   Reason: _____

   _____

   _____

6. Shipping coal from Minneapolis to New Orleans.

   Transportation mode: _____

   Reason: _____

Chapter 19 OUTLINE
Global Promotional Strategies

GLOBAL FOCUS: UNILEVER: AN ADVERTISING GIANT

LESSON 19-1 GLOBAL COMMUNICATIONS AND PROMOTIONS

THE COMMUNICATION PROCESS

INTERNATIONAL PROMOTIONAL ACTIVITIES

FOUR MAIN PROMOTIONAL ACTIVITIES

Advertising

Personal Selling

Publicity

Sales Promotion

THE INTERNATIONAL PROMOTIONAL MIX

LESSON FEATURE
A QUESTION OF ETHICS

LESSON 19-2 PLANNING GLOBAL ADVERTISING

ADVERTISING PLANNING PROCESS

STEP 1: ANALYZE TARGET MARKET

STEP 2: CREATE ADVERTISING MESSAGE

STEP 3: SELECT MEDIA

Newspaper Advertising

Television Advertising

Radio Advertising

Magazine Advertising

Direct Mail

Outdoor Advertising

Internet Advertising

STEP 4: EXECUTE AND EVALUATE

USING AN ADVERTISING AGENCY

LESSON FEATURE
E-COMMERCE IN ACTION: BANNERS, BUTTONS, AND E-MAIL BLASTS

LESSON 19-3 GLOBAL SELLING AND SALES PROMOTIONS

PERSONAL SELLING

PERSONAL SELLING ACTIVITIES

PERSONAL SELLING PROCESS

Step 1: Identify Customers

Step 2: Prepare a Presentation

Step 3: Obtain Feedback

Step 4: Close the Sale

Step 5: Provide Customer Service

PERSONAL SELLING IN INTERNATIONAL MARKETS

OTHER INTERNATIONAL PROMOTIONAL ACTIVITIES

PUBLIC RELATIONS

GLOBAL SALES PROMOTIONS

Coupons

Premiums

Contests and Sweepstakes

Point-of-Purchase Promotions

Specialty Advertising

LESSON FEATURES
GLOBAL BUSINESS EXAMPLE: COLGATE'S PROMOTIONAL EFFORTS IN THAILAND

REGIONAL PERSPECTIVE: CULTURE: PROMOTIONAL EFFORTS EXPAND SOCCER'S POPULARITY

Lesson 19-1
Global Communications and Promotions

LESSON QUIZ

Directions: For each of the following statements, if the statement is true, write a T on the answer line; if the statement is false, write an F on the answer line.

_____ 1. Noise helps improve the effectiveness of the communication process.

_____ 2. The communication process includes a source of a message, the medium used to carry the message, and the audience for the message.

_____ 3. Toll-free telephone numbers, e-mail, and web sites encourage customers to complete the communication process by giving feedback.

_____ 4. The primary difference between publicity and advertising is that a company does not pay for advertising.

_____ 5. Advertising involves personal, direct communication between sellers and potential customers.

_____ 6. Publicity is also referred to as *mass selling* because millions of people may see it.

_____ 7. The promotional mix may be different in different countries due to social, legal, and economic environments.

_____ 8. Advertising through the mail is effective in all countries.

_____ 9. Push promotions are directed at intermediaries in the distribution channel.

Directions: For each of the following items, decide which choice best completes the statement. Write the letter that identifies your choice on the answer line.

_____ 10. The communication process in which the source of a message puts the message in a form that the audience will understand is
A. encoding.
B. decoding.
C. medium.
D. feedback.

_____ 11. The four main promotional activities are
A. coupons, contests, free samples, and in-store displays.
B. television, radio, newspaper, and magazine advertisements.
C. advertising, personal selling, publicity, and sales promotion.
D. none of these

_____ 12. An example of a push promotion is
A. an advertisement in a consumer magazine.
B. a coupon.
C. a contest awarding a prize to the salesperson who sells the highest volume of a product during a specific time period.
D. none of these

Activity 1 • Analyzing Promotional Activity

Directions: For each of the following situations, use a check mark to indicate the type of promotional activity.

		Advertising	Personal Selling	Publicity	Sales Promotion
1.	A newspaper prints a recipe with brand name ingredients.				
2.	A person receives a telephone call about a credit card.				
3.	A television commercial is shown.				
4.	A television report tells about a company's recycling activities.				
5.	A company gives away T-shirts with a product picture.				
6.	A store clerk informs you about the features of a microwave oven.				

Activity 2 • Identifying Components of the Communication Process

Directions: Complete the diagram of the communication process with the following examples about a television commercial for athletic wear.

7. Television commercial
8. Viewer calls toll-free number for additional information
9. Telephone rings during television commercial
10. 23-year-old male views commercial
11. 18-35 year-old males
12. Athletic wear company
13. Advertising agency prepares commercial
14. "Get in Shape—Now"

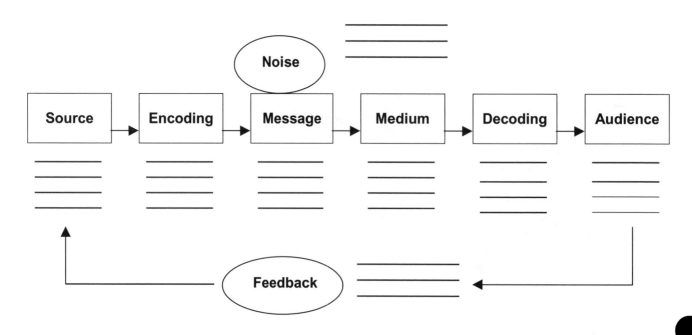

©South-Western Educational Publishing Chapter 19

Lesson 19-2
Planning Global Advertising

LESSON QUIZ

Directions: For each of the following statements, if the statement is true, write a T on the answer line; if the statement is false, write an F on the answer line.

_____ 1. Standardized advertising involves using one promotional approach in all geographic regions.

_____ 2. Some television channels are available to billions of viewers throughout the world.

_____ 3. Once a target market is analyzed, the advertising message should be tailored to that target market.

_____ 4. Many newspapers are posting their classified ads on the Internet; therefore, advertisers have the potential of advertising in two media at the same time.

_____ 5. In less-developed countries with a low per capita income and literacy rate, direct mail advertising is probably more suitable than other communication methods for advertising.

_____ 6. Database marketing uses computerized information systems to target their promotions to specific customers.

_____ 7. Lead times for advertising need to be adjusted depending on the media because each has different requirements.

_____ 8. Most multinational companies have their own advertising departments and do not use advertising agencies.

_____ 9. The research department of an advertising agency develops the content and artistic features of a message.

Directions: For each of the following items, decide which choice best completes the statement. Write the letter that identifies your choice on the answer line.

_____ 10. An advertising message that presents the quality, brand, price, or features of a product is
   A. a product quality ad.
   B. a comparative ad.
   C. a lifestyle ad.
   D. an endorsement ad.

_____ 11. An example of a lifestyle advertising approach would be a television commercial
   A. that uses a famous movie actor to recommend a product.
   B. that shows a young married couple using their microwave oven to cook popcorn.
   C. that emphasizes puppies and kittens while describing the product.
   D. none of these

_____ 12. In an advertising agency, the department that is the link between the agency and the client is the
   A. research department.
   B. creative department.
   C. account services department.
   D. media department.

Activity 1 • Identifying Common Advertising Techniques

Directions: Based on your experience with television, magazine, and newspaper advertisements, describe an example of each of the following promotional techniques.

1. Product quality ads _____

_____

2. Comparative ads _____

_____

3. Emotional ads _____

_____

4. Humorous ads _____

_____

5. Lifestyle ads _____

_____

6. Endorsement ads _____

_____

Activity 2 • Determining Advertising Media for International Promotions

Directions: For each of the following situations, write in the media type that would best serve the company and give reasons for your selection.

Media

newspaper	direct mail
magazine	radio
television	outdoor

7. To advertise to people while driving, a company should use _____

Reason _____

_____

8. To attract customers who are not home at regular times, a company should use _____

_____

Reason _____

_____

9. To advertise to young consumers interested in sports, a company should use _____

Reason _____

_____

10. To promote a product in a country with very little broadcast media, a company should use _____

_____

Reason _____

_____

 ©South-Western Educational Publishing

Lesson 19-3
Global Selling and Sales Promotions

LESSON QUIZ

Directions: For each of the following statements, if the statement is true, write a T on the answer line; if the statement is false, write an F on the answer line.

_____ 1. Personal selling occurs only when the seller and the customer meet face-to-face.

_____ 2. Telemarketing is used in selling because it often provides fast, low-cost contacts.

_____ 3. The personal selling process starts with preparing the sales presentation.

_____ 4. Once a successful sales presentation is developed, it should be used exactly the same with all potential customers.

_____ 5. One way to overcome customer objections in a personal selling presentation is to offer a lower price to compromise some feature the customer does not like.

_____ 6. Personal selling ends when the sale is closed.

_____ 7. When a multinational company uses local nationals for personal selling, the training usually emphasizes product knowledge.

_____ 8. When a company makes charitable contributions it is engaging in public relations to create a positive image of the company.

_____ 9. The only reason a company sponsors a contest or sweepstakes is to draw attention to its products.

_____10. Companies may use public relations to gain or maintain a favorable public image.

Directions: For each of the following items, decide which choice best completes the statement. Write the letter that identifies your choice on the answer line.

_____11. All of the following could be used in an effective personal selling presentation except
   A. offering a test drive of a new automobile to demonstrate its features.
   B. presenting a chart listing well-known people who use the product.
   C. demonstrating how to use the word processing software product to create a document.
   D. advertising the product in a community newspaper.

_____12. Follow-up contacts, advance notices of special sales, and frequent-buyer programs are examples of
   A. a personal selling sales presentation.
   B. public relations.
   C. relationship marketing.
   D. closing a sale.

_____13. All of the following are examples of sales promotions except
   A. sponsoring a Little League team.
   B. offering a toy with a purchase of the company's product.
   C. attaching coupon dispensers on grocery store shelves.
   D. distributing calendars that describe the company and its products.

Activity 1 • Preparing a Sales Presentation

Directions: Answer the questions below to prepare a personal selling sales presentation for the following scenario. You may add details to complete the sales presentation.

Scenario: Your company has just designed and produced a line of computers that are low-priced, especially in quantity, and are ideal for networked systems. Your territory consists of companies that have fewer than 100 employees.

1. How will you identify customers?

   _____

   _____

   _____

2. Who would you call to set up an appointment for a sales presentation?

   _____

   _____

   _____

3. Describe the sales presentation you would make.

   _____

   _____

   _____

   _____

   _____

   _____

   _____

   _____

4. What are two objections you might encounter and how would you respond to them?

   _____

   _____

   _____

   _____

   _____

   _____

5. What are two questions you could ask to close the sale?

   _____

   _____

   _____

   _____

©South-Western Educational Publishing

Chapter 20 OUTLINE
Global Financial Activities

GLOBAL FOCUS: KOOR INDUSTRIES, LTD.

LESSON 20-1 FINANCING GLOBAL BUSINESS OPERATIONS

INTERNATIONAL FLOW OF FUNDS

SOURCES OF FUNDS

Equity Capital

Debt Capital

USES OF FUNDS

Current Expenses

Long-Term Costs

GLOBAL FINANCIAL INSTITUTIONS

DEPOSIT-TYPE FINANCIAL INSTITUTIONS

Commercial Banks

Savings and Loan Associations

Credit Unions

OTHER TYPES OF FINANCIAL INSTITUTIONS

Mutual Fund

Life Insurance Company

 ©South-Western Educational Publishing

LESSON FEATURES
GLOBAL BUSINESS EXAMPLE: THE TECHIMAN WOMEN'S MARKET CREDIT UNION

E-COMMERCE IN ACTION: CYBER BANKS

LESSON 20-2 GLOBAL FINANCIAL MARKETS

GLOBAL STOCK MARKETS

MAJOR STOCK EXCHANGES

THE STOCK MARKET IN ACTION

STOCK MARKET PRICE INFORMATION

LESSON FEATURE
GLOBAL BUSINESS EXAMPLE: THE PRAGUE STOCK EXCHANGE

LESSON 20-3 INTERNATIONAL FINANCIAL MARKETS

THE BOND MARKET

CORPORATE BONDS

GOVERNMENT BONDS

Federal Government Bonds

State and Local Government Bonds

OTHER FINANCIAL MARKETS

THE OVER-THE-COUNTER MARKET

FOREIGN EXCHANGE MARKET

FUTURES MARKET

LESSON FEATURES
GLOBAL BUSINESS EXAMPLE: ARE ALL JUNK BONDS GARBAGE?

REGIONAL PERSPECTIVE: HISTORY: THE GULF WAR OF 1991

©South-Western Educational Publishing

COMMUNICATION ACROSS BORDERS: THE CHAMELEON-LIKE SAUDI ARABIAN FINANCIERS

LESSON 20-4 ANALYZING INTERNATIONAL INVESTMENTS

INVESTMENT GOALS

CURRENT INCOME

LONG-TERM GROWTH

GLOBAL INVESTMENT OPPORTUNITIES

IDENTIFYING POTENTIAL INVESTMENTS

EVALUATING INVESTMENT OPPORTUNITIES

Rate of Return

Liquidity

Taxes

Safety

INVESTMENT INFORMATION SOURCES

NEWS MEDIA

INTERNET

FINANCIAL EXPERTS

INVESTMENT INFORMATION SERVICES

LESSON FEATURE
GLOBAL BUSINESS EXAMPLE: ONLINE INVESTING

©South-Western Educational Publishing

Chapter 21 OUTLINE
Managing International Business Ris

GLOBAL FOCUS: LLOYD'S OF LONDON

LESSON 21-1 GLOBAL RISK MANAGEMENT

INTERNATIONAL BUSINESS RISKS

POLITICAL RISK

SOCIAL RISK

ECONOMIC RISK

MONITORING GLOBAL BUSINESS RISK

THE RISK MANAGEMENT PROCESS

STEP 1—IDENTIFY POTENTIAL RISKS

STEP 2—EVALUATE RISKS

STEP 3—SELECT A RISK MANAGE   METHOD

Risk Avoida

Risk Reduction

Risk Assumption

Risk Sharing

STEP 4—IMPLEMENT THE RISK MANAGEMENT PROGRAM

LESSON FEATURES
GLOBAL BUSINESS EXAMPLE: PRACTICING FOR UNEXPECTED EVENTS

A QUESTION OF ETHICS: UNREPORTED BUSINESS ACTIVITIES

LESSON 21-2 INTERNATIONAL INSURANCE

INSURING AGAINST RISKS

INSURABLE INTEREST

INSURABLE RISK

INSURANCE POLICY ELEMENTS

DECLARATION

INSURING AGREEMENT

CONDITIONS

EXCLUSIONS

ENDORSEMENT

LESSON FEATURES
GLOBAL BUSINESS EXAMPLE: AIG IN CHINA

REGIONAL PERSPECTIVE: HISTORY: THE ORGANIZATION OF PETROLEUM EXPORTING COUNTRIES

LESSON 21-3 REDUCING GLOBAL RISKS

GLOBAL INSURANCE COVERAGES

MARINE INSURANCE

PROPERTY INSURANCE

Loss of Real Property

Loss of Personal Property

Financial Responsibility for Injuries or Damage

THE OVERSEAS PRIVATE INVESTMENT CORPORATION

CREDIT RISK INSURANCE

RISK REDUCTION FOR GLOBAL BUSINESS

Conduct Business in Many Countries

Diversify Product Offerings

Involve Local Ownership

Employ Local Management

LESSON FEATURES

COMMUNICATION ACROSS BORDERS: NOT ALL LANGUAGES ARE EQUAL FOR BUSINESS PURPOSES

GLOBAL BUSINESS EXAMPLE: THE RUSSIAN INSURANCE INDUSTRY

Lesson 21-1
Global Risk Management

LESSON QUIZ

Directions: For each of the following statements, if the statement is true, write a T on the answer line; if the statement is false, write an F on the answer line.

_____ 1. Political risks are commonly affected by family-work relationships in a country.

_____ 2. Global companies can assess risk fairly easily when the government is unstable.

_____ 3. One risk that occurs when there is civil unrest or revolution in a country is the risk of a change in the government that changes the business climate for global companies.

_____ 4. Low inflation increases the economic risk of doing business in a country.

_____ 5. When a country begins to experience high rates of unemployment, businesses are at risk because people will have less money to buy their products.

_____ 6. Business should constantly monitor conditions in a country because the ability to anticipate and act early can reduce risk and lessen the chances of poor business decisions.

_____ 7. When the business environment in a country changes, the change affects all companies doing business in that country in the same way.

_____ 8. A company that tries to avoid risk by only selling in its home country is also limiting its potential for expansion.

_____ 9. With self-insurance a company takes responsibility for losses from certain risks.

Directions: For each of the following items, decide which choice best completes the statement. Write the letter that identifies your choice on the answer line.

_____ 10. Three common risks faced by companies in international business are
   A. political, social, and economic risk.
   B. political, competitive, and inflation risks.
   C. economic, religious, and inflation risks.
   D. none of these

_____ 11. Packaging laws, antidumping laws, and currency exchange controls are examples of
   A. social risks.
   B. economic risks.
   C. political risks.
   D. all of these

_____ 12. Implementing a risk management program involves
   A. selecting a risk management method.
   B. executing the risk management methods selected and measuring the success of the actions.
   C. analyzing the potential risks that have been identified.
   D. none of these

Activity 1 • Analyzing International Business Risks

Directions: For each of the following situations, place a check mark in the appropriate column to identify whether the situation is an example of a political risk, social risk, or economic risk.

		Political Risk	Social Risk	Economic Risk
1.	Changes in consumer spending in a nation due to reduced employment opportunities			
2.	New business regulations that require all food packages to list the potential dangers of ingredients			
3.	Religious beliefs in a country that do not allow people to eat certain foods			
4.	A trade deficit of a nation that reduces the value of its currency			
5.	Traditions in a country that encourage family members to work for the family business			
6.	Frequent changes in the government ruling party in a nation			
7.	Import taxes that discourage buying foreign-made goods			
8.	Changes in the buying power of a nation's currency			

Activity 2 • Analyzing Risk Management Methods

Directions: Write the letters identifying the risk management methods on the answer lines to identify which method is being used in each of the situations that follow.

Risk Management Method

RAV Risk avoidance

RR   Risk reduction

RAS Risk assumption

RS   Risk sharing

_____ 9. A Brazilian company decides to build factories only in countries that allow foreign businesses to have total control of assets.

_____ 10. A South African company buys property insurance with fire coverage for its factories in other countries.

_____ 11. A multinational company requires that its workers know a foreign language and understand different cultures.

_____ 12. A Cambodian entrepreneur sets aside money to cover financial losses.

_____ 13. An Israeli company uses a monitoring system to prevent stealing by customers and employees.

_____ 14. A German company buys currency futures to avoid losses on exchange rates.

    ©South-Western Educational Publishing

Lesson 21-2
International Insurance

LESSON QUIZ

Directions: For each of the following statements, if the statement is true, write a T on the answer line; if the statement is false, write an F on the answer line.

_____ 1. Insurance is a means of sharing losses among many people.

_____ 2. A stock insurance company is owned by its policyholders and returns any surplus to policyholders.

_____ 3. An insurance company will generally not issue insurance for a risk that is faced by only one person or business.

_____ 4. In order to calculate the cost of providing insurance coverage, an insurance company must be able to calculate the probability that the risk will occur.

_____ 5. An insurable risk must be able to be documented.

_____ 6. An insurance policy is a contract.

_____ 7. The reason companies are willing to include a deductible in an insurance policy is that deductibles lower the premium.

_____ 8. A deductible is property or a risk that is not covered by an insurance policy.

Directions: For each of the following items, decide which choice best completes the statement. Write the letter that identifies your choice on the answer line.

_____ 9. If an insurance policy states that the insurance will not cover the first $500 of loss, the $500 is
   A. an exclusion.
   B. a deductible.
   C. a premium.
   D. an endorsement.

_____ 10. If a company wishes to remove a factory that has been sold from its insurance policy, the insurance policy would need to have
   A. an exclusion.
   B. a deductible.
   C. a premium.
   D. an endorsement.

_____ 11. All of the following risks would be considered insurable risks except
   A. the injury to a customer on company property.
   B. the damage to computer equipment from an office fire.
   C. an unexpected increase in the cost of office supplies.
   D. the death of company executives in an airplane crash.

Activity 1 • Identifying Insurance Policy Elements

Directions: For each of the statements that follow, write the letter identifying the insurance policy element.

Insurance Policy Elements

A. Deductible   E. Insurable risk
B. Endorsement   F. Insured
C. Exclusion   G. Insurer
D. Insurable interest   H. Premium

_____ 1. "Coverage does not include losses due to war or civil disturbances."

_____ 2. "Insurance is provided for the Kenton Exporting Co."

_____ 3. "The cost of insurance for one year is $4,500."

_____ 4. "All losses must be documented with legal proof of loss due to fire or theft."

_____ 5. "The first $500 of all claims will be paid by the insured."

_____ 6. "Coverage is for the 23-story office building in Paris."

_____ 7. "Coverage is provided by the Global Mutual Insurance Company."

_____ 8. "The company no longer owns the factory in Egypt; this property is no longer covered."

Activity 2 • Identifying Insurable Risks

Directions: For each of the statements that follow, explain why the risk is insurable or not insurable. Use the elements of insurable risk as your reasons.

9. Everyone who lives and works in London, England dies in a nuclear attack. _____

_____

_____

10. A company wishes to insure against the possibility that a meeting will be delayed by a late arrival.

_____

_____

11. A company wants insurance for its fleet of vehicles. _____

_____

_____

12. A father wants insurance that his daughter will be admitted to the college of her choice. _____

_____

_____

13. A global company wants to insure against loss of its factories in other countries due to expropriation occurring when a government changes. _____

_____

_____

14. A company wants to insure a shipment of goods to another country. _____

_____

_____

 ©South-Western Educational Publishing

Lesson 21-3
Reducing Global Risks

LESSON QUIZ

Directions: For each of the following statements, if the statement is true, write a T on the answer line; if the statement is false, write an F on the answer line.

_____ 1. When goods are shipped overseas, the ship owner is responsible for the goods and any insurance against their loss or damage.

_____ 2. Ocean marine insurance covers the risk of shipping goods on inland waterways, railroad lines, truck lines, and airlines.

_____ 3. All-risk marine insurance coverage includes all losses except those associated with war.

_____ 4. The most expensive type of marine insurance is all-risk coverage.

_____ 5. Real property refers to office buildings, stores, factories, and warehouses.

_____ 6. Employers cannot be held responsible for the actions of their employees.

_____ 7. OPIC insurance can protect a company from a foreign government's refusal to convert its currency to dollars.

_____ 8. Not receiving payment for merchandise is a risk of doing business.

_____ 9. The Foreign Credit Insurance Association provides credit risk insurance.

_____10. A global business can reduce its risk by doing business in many countries.

Directions: For each of the following items, decide which choice best completes the statement. Write the letter that identifies your choice on the answer line.

_____11. Personal property includes all of the following except
    A. a computer network.
    B. a garage.
    C. office furniture.
    D. the inventory in a clothing store.

_____12. OPIC insurance can cover financial losses due to all of the following except
    A. inconvertibility.
    B. shipping losses.
    C. political unrest.
    D. expropriation.

_____13. Global businesses can reduce business risk by all of the following methods except
    A. operating in many different countries to spread the risk around.
    B. offering one standardized product to reduce development and promotion investments.
    C. offering many different goods and services.
    D. employing local managers.

Activity 1 • Identifying Global Insurance Coverage

Directions: Name the type of insurance that a company would use for each of the following risk situations.

1. Shipping automobiles by water from Japan to Australia. _____

   _____

2. Selling to companies in other countries that may not pay for delivered goods. _____

   _____

3. Insurance for loss of tools, office furniture, and computers. _____

   _____

4. Loss of assets in a foreign country when seized by the host government. _____

   _____

5. Shipping goods by railroad across Europe. _____

   _____

6. A customer is injured by a product manufactured by a foreign company. _____

   _____

Activity 2 • Planning for Global Risk

Directions: Read the following scenario and then describe what risks are involved and what risk procedures the company should take.

Scenario: Hexiplex Company has its home office in the United States and operates factories and stores in several Central and South American countries. In one small country, General Roderigo Perez heads the army and is popular with both the military and the citizens of the country. Company analysts suggest that the general is corrupt and greedy and that he takes bribes and operates a drug network. He has become wealthy and analysts fear he will soon stage a coup and take over the government. What are the risks to the company and what actions should the company take to plan for the risks?

_____

_____

_____

_____

_____

_____

_____

_____

_____

_____

_____

_____

_____

Supplemental Forms

MAKING ETHICAL DECISIONS

Description of decision to be made _____

_____

Is the action legal? (Consider laws in both the home country and countries affected by the decision.) _____

_____

Does the action violate professional or company standards? _____

_____

Who is affected by the action and how? (Use the grid below to identify the parties affected and how they are affected.)

Company (finances, employees, owners, etc.)	Society (environment, economy, safety and health, etc.)	Consumers	Competitors

MAKING ETHICAL DECISIONS

Description of decision to be made _____

_____

Is the action legal? (Consider laws in both the home country and countries affected by the decision.) _____

_____

_____

Does the action violate professional or company standards? _____

_____

_____

Who is affected by the action and how? (Use the grid below to identify the parties affected and how they are affected.)

Company (finances, employees, owners, etc.)	Society (environment, economy, safety and health, etc.)	Consumers	Competitors

©South-Western Educational Publishing   Supplemental Forms

THE DECISION-MAKING PROCESS

1. Define the problem. (What do I need or want?)

_____

_____

_____

2. Identify the alternatives. (What are the different ways my problem can be solved?)

_____

_____

_____

_____

3. Evaluate the alternatives. (What are the advantages and disadvantages of each of the choices available? Use the decision matrix on the back of this page to list and evaluate the alternatives.)

_____

_____

_____

4. Make a choice. (Based on the advantages and disadvantages, which would be my best choice? Can I live with the consequences of that choice?)

_____

_____

_____

_____

5. Take action on the choice. (What needs to be done to put the decision into action?)

_____

_____

_____

_____

6. Review the decision. (Did your decision solve the problem? As time goes by, what different actions might be necessary? Were there consequences you did not predict when you evaluated the alternatives?)

_____

_____

_____

_____

DECISION MATRIX

Alternatives (describe)	Advantages	Disadvantages
Alternative No. 1		
Alternative No. 2		
Alternative No. 3		
Alternative No. 4		
Alternative No. 5		

©South-Western Educational Publishing

RESUME PLANNER

1. Personal Data (full name, address, phone, fax, e-mail, home page URL) _____

_____

_____

_____

2. Type of job _____

_____

_____

3. Objective (stated to match type of job described) _____

_____

_____

_____

_____

4. Experience (job title, duties, dates of employment, employers' names and addresses) _____

_____

_____

_____

_____

_____

_____

_____

_____

_____

_____

5. Related activities (school activities, hobbies, other interests directly related to type of job) _____

_____

_____

_____

_____

_____

_____

_____

_____

_____

_____

6. Education (schools attended, dates, fields of study, relevant courses or programs) _____

_____

_____

_____

_____

_____

_____

_____

7. Honors and awards (that indicate ability to do high-quality work) _____

_____

_____

_____

_____

_____

_____

_____

_____

8. References (name, address, telephone number, position/relationship) _____

_____

_____

_____

_____

_____

_____

_____

_____

_____

_____

   ©South-Western Educational Publishing   Supplemental Forms

ANALYZING BUSINESS NEWS

Directions: Locate a recent newspaper or magazine article that discusses some aspect of international business. Provide the article information and answer the questions that follow. If possible, attach the article or a copy of it to this sheet.

Title of article _____

Author _____

Source of article _____

Date _____

1. Topic area—Describe the global business elements the article refers to.

    _____

    _____

    _____

2. Is the source of the article a reliable source? Explain why or why not.

    _____

    _____

    _____

3. Write a two- or three-sentence summary of the main facts of the article.

    _____

    _____

    _____

    _____

    _____

4. What is the author's main point?

    _____

    _____

    _____

5. Who is affected by the situation described in the article, and how?

    _____

    _____

    _____

    _____

    _____

    _____

    _____

6. How is the information in the article relevant to you?

_____

_____

_____

_____

_____

_____

_____

7. Do you agree with the author's opinion or with the actions described in the article? Why or why not?

_____

_____

_____

_____

_____

_____

_____

_____

8. If you wanted to find additional information about this topic, what key words would you use to search the Internet?

_____

_____

_____

9. What additional questions do you have about this topic?

_____

_____

_____

_____

_____

_____

_____

©South-Western Educational Publishing
Supplemental Forms

MARKETING PLAN

Directions: Create an imaginary new product for your imaginary company and outline the marketing plan for this product.

Description of Product _____

_____

_____

_____

_____

1. Company Goals

   _____

   _____

   _____

   _____

   _____

   _____

   _____

   _____

2. Description of Customers and Their Needs

   _____

   _____

   _____

   _____

   _____

   _____

   _____

   _____

3. Information about Competitors

   _____

   _____

   _____

   _____

   _____

   _____

   _____

   _____

4. Information about Economic, Social, Legal, and Technological Trends

_____

_____

_____

_____

_____

_____

_____

5. Financial and Human Resources Available

_____

_____

_____

_____

_____

_____

_____

6. Time Line of Actions to Be Taken

_____

_____

_____

_____

_____

_____

_____

7. Methods for Measuring Success

_____

_____

_____

_____

_____

_____

_____